Restoring Harmony

A Guide for Managing Conflicts in Schools

James L. Lee
University of Wisconsin

Charles J. Pulvino
University of Wisconsin

Philip A. Perrone
University of Wisconsin

Merrill, an imprint of Prentice Hall
Upper Saddle River, New Jersey   Columbus, Ohio

Library of Congress Cataloging-in-Publication Data

Lee, James L.

    Restoring harmony : a guide for managing conflicts in schools / James L. Lee,
Charles J. Pulvino, Philip A. Perrone

        p. cm.

    Includes bibliographical references and index.

    ISBN: 0-13-470313-8

    1. Classroom management. 2. School violence—Prevention. 3. Conflict management.
4. Counseling in education.   I. Pulvino, Charles J. II. Perrone, Philip A. III. Title.

    LB3013.L44   1998

    371.5'8—dc21

                              96-53393

                                   CIP

Editor: Kevin M. Davis
Production Editor: Christine M. Harrington
Design Coordinator: Karrie M. Converse
Text Designer: Ed Horcharik
Cover Designer: Russ Maselli
Production Manager: Deidra M. Schwartz
Electronic Text Management: Marilyn Wilson Phelps, Matthew Williams, Karen L. Bretz,
   Tracey B. Ward
Illustrations: Tom Kennedy
Director of Marketing: Kevin Flanagan
Advertising/Marketing Coordinator: Julie Shough

This book was set in Garamond by Prentice Hall and was printed and bound by Book Press.
The cover was printed by Phoenix Color Corp.

 © 1998 by Prentice-Hall, Inc.
Simon & Schuster/A Viacom Company
Upper Saddle River, New Jersey 07458

Printed in the United States of America

10 9 8 7 6 5 4 3 2 1

ISBN: 0-13-470313-8

Prentice-Hall International (UK) Limited, *London*
Prentice-Hall of Australia Pty. Limited, *Sydney*
Prentice-Hall of Canada, Inc., *Toronto*
Prentice-Hall Hispanoamericana, S. A., *Mexico*
Prentice-Hall of India Private Limited, *New Delhi*
Prentice-Hall of Japan, Inc., *Tokyo*
Simon & Schuster Asia Pte. Ltd., *Singapore*
Editora Prentice-Hall do Brasil, Ltda., *Rio de Janeiro*

We dedicate this book to schoolteachers, whose hard work, perseverance, and dedication prepare the nation's youth for success in a changing environment. We applaud teachers for their continuous, unselfish efforts.

Preface

Conflict, or the potential for conflict, is obvious to anyone intimately involved with schools. Schoolchildren are faced daily with confrontations, threats, and physical and psychological badgering. Teachers are increasingly confronted with students who undervalue education and who behave in a hostile, aggressive, or belligerent manner. Parents who want the best for their children, yet are disassociated from the school, place seemingly unrealistic demands on teachers. Administrators who try to balance demands of parents and needs of teachers frequently fail to satisfy either. Given this picture, one that is all too accurate in many schools, is it any wonder that teachers could benefit from a text that specifically addresses conflict management? We think not.

This text is written for practicing teachers and teachers in training. It offers these professionals ways to think about and manage conflict that they observe and experience. The foundation for the material presented here comes from three separate sources. First, experience gained from being in the school environment provides the primary source of information. We three authors have been teachers most of our professional lives. We all have extensive public school classroom teaching experience and experience in public schools as counselors, supervisors, and consultants. Second, psychological literature accounts for a meaningful source of information. All three of us have doctorates in counseling psychology and extensive experience in applying counseling principles in school settings. Finally, the Japanese martial art aikido furnishes a theoretical foundation. One of us has earned a second-degree black belt in this discipline, another has practiced and studied aikido doctrine, and the third has served to keep the others from getting "carried away."

We believe that the "gentle martial art" of aikido, with its emphasis on *restoring harmony,* is an appropriate basis for managing conflict in school settings. We present educational management strategies that emanate from psychological sources and embrace principles from aikido. These strategies emphasize theoretical foundations and practical applications in school settings. We provide teacher-student dialogues to demonstrate applications of strategies. In addition, we cite bibliographic sources and resources for readers interested in furthering their knowledge of conflict management.

We value schools and schoolteachers. Their job is a difficult one and one of the most important in society. Yet it is a job that all too frequently goes underresourced, unrewarded, underpaid, and unappreciated. We believe that teachers will be able to do a better job of educating youth when society realizes the yeoman task they face and supplies them sufficient resources to accomplish society's educational goals. Until that happens, teachers need information to help them reduce and/or manage conflict so that they can maximize educational outcomes. We believe that the present text, *Restoring Harmony: A Guide for Managing Conflicts in Schools,* provides pertinent, specific, helpful information that teachers can use to accomplish their difficult task in a way that satisfactorily manages conflict.

ACKNOWLEDGMENTS

We sincerely appreciate the assistance of the following people who reviewed the manuscript and provided constructive feedback for changes: Lowell J. Bethel, University of Texas, Austin; Nils S. Carlson, Jr., California State University, Bakersfield; Leslie J. Chamberlin, Bowling Green State University; and Dorothy Dobson, Utah State University.

Brief Contents

Contents

CHAPTER 8

Managing Schools and Classrooms to Minimize Disruptive Behavior   123

CHAPTER 9

Dealing with Multiple-Person Conflicts   141

CHAPTER 10

Mediating Conflicts   151

CHAPTER 11

Developing a Peer Mediation Program   159

CHAPTER 12

Getting the Most Out of Your Students   173

Index   189

CHAPTER 1

The Nature of Conflict

Imagine the following situation.

It is Parents' Night at school in early October. A sixth-grade teacher, Mr. Rich, begins to address a room full of parents, when a parent, obviously very upset, stands up and begins to criticize him because of his teaching style and classroom organization. The parent's comments concern the modern methods that Mr. Rich has been using. The parent wants Mr. Rich to return to the basics and stop all the fancy stuff.

> PARENT: Mr. Rich, I don't think what you are doing with this open classroom stuff is going to teach my son or other people's kids the basics they need to succeed in school. Why should students help set their own goals? Whatever happened to the good old-fashioned reading, writing, and arithmetic?

By noticing the head nods of other parents, Mr. Rich realizes that they share similar feelings. Other parents remain silent. Still others seem embarrassed by this one parent's outburst. If you were Mr. Rich, what would you do?

- Change the subject?
- Begin explaining your philosophy of teaching and education?
- Remain silent until the parent finished and then continue with your prepared presentation?
- Try to negotiate with the complaining parent and others about how to run the classroom?
- Acknowledge the parent's right to feel and think that way and begin a discussion among those in attendance concerning the remarks of the complaining parent?
- Become flustered and leave the room?

Each of these responses is a way of dealing with the conflict activated by the disturbed parent. Each of these possible responses may be appropriate. Each response has strengths, weaknesses, and consequences to consider. As concepts are developed in several succeeding chapters, this example and the various possible responses to the conflict will be reviewed, repeated, and discussed. In addition, a number of ways Mr. Rich could respond in the situation will be presented.

CONFLICT IN OUR SCHOOLS

Conflict in schools occurs in a variety of ways. It arises between parents and teachers, as in the previous example. Students argue with teachers and administrators. Students argue with each other. Sometimes conflicts lead to physical violence. In some cities police officers have been assigned to schools to help prevent physical conflicts. Students have been discovered carrying firearms and knives to school for self-protection and to attack other students. Teachers have been verbally and physically attacked by students. Teachers have sometimes physically and sexually abused students. We do not condone or excuse any of these forms of conflict, yet they exist.

Every teacher and student have experienced conflict in a variety of ways and a variety of situations within school environments. Conflict is part of life in schools and in society in general. The amount of conflict and violence in schools varies in intensity from rural to urban settings. However, no community, large or small, rural or urban, has escaped the effects of conflict.

A number of hypotheses have been forwarded as to why such conflict exists. In various ways, any or all of the following factors have been blamed for the amount of rising conflict and violence in our schools:

Economic factors—The current level of poverty in our country and the diminishing purchasing power for the middle class contribute to inequalities that become the source of irritation and conflict.

Media—The level and intensity of violence on television, in movies, and in music are often cited as providing a foundation for the easy acceptance and even promotion of violence as a way of resolving conflict.

Breakdown in family values—The increase in child care centers, latchkey children, and unsupervised baby-sitters are blamed for children developing without a sense of obligation and responsibility to *normal* family values.

Conflict of educational approaches—Some people want schools to teach values— right and wrong—and others have the more permissive attitude that students need to discover those concepts themselves.

Drugs and alcohol—Student use of drugs, students selling drugs, and the territorial wars about selling and distributing drugs are all sources of conflict within and near schools.

And so on. . . .

Although various political, social, and religious leaders have emphasized one or more of these reasons as a primary cause of conflict and resulting violence, probably all of them contribute in varying degrees to the rising tide of conflict in society and schools.

How we manage conflict depends on our understanding and approach to conflict. The next sections describe several ways of thinking about conflict and harmony.

HARMONY

The typical understanding of harmony is the absence of conflict, a peaceful situation, and calm atmosphere. However, from our point of view, harmony is not the absence of conflict but the restoration of balance among opposing energies (Crum, 1987). A look at nature can help us understand this perspective. Weather highs (good weather) are usually balanced by weather lows (bad or rainy weather). When the balance between weather highs and lows is disturbed, the result is thunder storms, tornadoes, or hurricanes. Thus, in nature, harmony is not the absence of conflict but the balance of energies. This balance maintains order. Conflict is a natural process, not to be avoided but to be managed in a productive way.

CONFLICT IS NATURAL

To begin to understand the nature of conflict, we can again look to nature. Within nature, conflict is a normal occurrence. The beauty of a mountain stream is built on rocks and stones that cause turbulence in the water's flow—a form of conflict. Also, survival of the fittest depends on natural competition and natural selection. This competition and selection frequently exhibit elements of conflict. Nature attempts to maintain balance through conflict among competing species. For example, despite some peoples' natural aversion to deer hunting each year, deer herds need to be harvested to maintain balance in nature. Before the advent of large cities, metropolitan areas, and highly cultivated rural areas, this process occurred naturally. However, because of population growth and the reduction of predators such as wolves, coyotes, and mountain lions that kept deer herds in balance, present deer populations continue to grow. Consequently, if people did not harvest deer herds through controlled hunting seasons, the deer population would grow out of control and damage life-supporting agricultural crops. As a result, many deer would die of starvation or fall victim to accidents.

In the human condition, conflict occurs because of many differences in naturally occurring phenomena. Some of the most obvious differences include but are not limited to the following:

Gender differences—Naturally occurring differences exist between males and females, particularly in regard to differences in communication styles (Tannen, 1990). These differences often lead to misunderstanding and conflict.

Ethnic differences—Cultural histories, contexts, and teachings promote differences in values, attitudes, and perceptions (Hall, 1981). These differences often lead to misunderstandings that, in turn, produce intolerance of one group for another (racism)—all sources of conflict.

Age differences—Age differences among people stimulate different perspectives (Strauss & Howe, 1991). These differences in values, attitudes, and perceptions among generations often lead to difficulty understanding and accepting each other's perspectives, which may produce conflict.

Physical size differences—Larger, stronger people have physical resources not available to smaller, weaker people. Although these differences in physical resources usually do not *cause* conflict, superior strength is frequently exploited in attempting to resolve conflicts.

Social economic class differences—A natural tension exists among people with economic resources and those without (Batra, 1987). This situation frequently leads to conflicts when individuals without resources seek to obtain resources at the expense of people who control those resources.

Status and role differences—Personal power is related to social roles. Parents are expected to manage their children's behavior. Teachers are supposed to be in charge of their classrooms. Managers should be in charge of their employees. Some people do not accept status and role differences as a basis for controlling behavior. This failure is a potential source of conflict.

Differences like these are normal and naturally occurring. The source of conflicts usually reside within people and their expectations of how others should behave. Usually, expectations are that others should act, talk, and perceive in certain ways within particular social contexts (e.g., not skateboarding through the shopping mall). When people do not act in expected ways, conflict often results. Some conflicts are created when people expect others to think and act the way they do. It is as if these people believe there is only one way of seeing the world—their way!

The processes leading to conflict are all natural. Conflict is not to be resolved or eliminated but to be expected and managed. We believe that conflict should be expected, recognized, and managed in productive ways that restore harmonious balance—when each person's rights are recognized and individual differences are acknowledged and/or accepted. With the complexity of people's perceptions and various contexts, the potential for conflict is nearly infinite.

Conflict is normal and a natural part of life (Markova, 1991). Therefore, it should not be viewed as a contest, in which a winner and a loser eventually emerge. When conflict is viewed as a contest, emotions and differences are intensified usually because one party gets rewarded at the expense of another. When this occurs, gains and losses are momentary. The one who loses is likely to perpetuate the conflict in the hope that in the future she or he will be victorious. By contrast, if conflict is viewed not as a contest but rather as a natural part of life, then having winners and losers is not relevant or important. All involved parties can, and should be, benefactors of the process. Remember, conflict just is! It is not to be avoided, run from, or fought against. It is to be acknowledged, accepted, utilized, and managed to restore the balance of harmony. Very often the process of trying to avoid and eliminate conflict intensifies it and results in those involved becoming less than they were before the conflict.

Perhaps several examples may clarify how attempting to avoid or eliminate conflict can intensify it. Consider the following student interaction on the playground:

JACK: *[sixth-grade student]* Hey, kid! Come here!

BOBBY: *[fourth-grade student] [Trying to avoid conflict, puts his head down and continues to walk away]*

JACK: Hey, I'm talking to you. Come here.

BOBBY: *[Continues to walk away]*

JACK: *[Runs to get in front of Bobby and shoves him backward on the shoulders]* Hey, I'm talking to you. Now what are you going to do?

Bobby's attempt to avoid conflict increased the conflict and ended in a physical confrontation. A second common example is when one student confronts another and the first student runs to a teacher in an attempt to eliminate the potential conflict. The result is that the first student accosts the second student later for being a tattle-tale or snitch. The very attempt to eliminate the conflict produces potentially more.

In later chapters, we will discuss a variety of ways that situations might be handled to manage the conflict and move toward harmony.

In conflict situations, the most important issue is how one manages to move toward balance and harmony. Managing conflict is rarely about who is right or wrong. Rather, balance and harmony is about acknowledgment, acceptance, and appreciation of differences. Because conflict is natural, not a contest, and results from naturally occurring differences, it is what one does with conflict that determines the outcome. The focus here is to learn to manage conflict to move toward balance and harmony.

A METAPHOR FOR RESTORING HARMONY

Throughout this book, we use principles and concepts from the Japanese martial art aikido. Aikido provides a foundation for understanding and managing conflict and for moving toward the balance of harmony. The connection between aikido, a martial art, and harmonious conflict management might seem contradictory. We hope to dispel this apparent contradiction. The public depictions of martial arts in the movies or on television often contain misrepresentations of both form and intent. The **form** has been dramatically distorted in fighting sequences carefully choreographed solely for entertainment purposes. The high-flying kicks, spinning backhand punches, and devastating arm bars usually would not occur in a street fight. As evidence, professional and amateur karate matches look more like boxing matches in which participants are *required* to use a minimum number of kicks each round. The choreographed fighting sequences reinforce a machismo view of martial arts as being aggressive rather than expressive disciplines. The distortion of **intent** amounts to a disregard of the martial arts' spiritual and ethical foundations. The martial arts are most often depicted as the most expedient method for conflict resolution to be invoked casually or even gratuitously (Fuller, 1988).

Morihei Ueshiba developed aikido in the early 1900s. Aikido was the culmination of Ueshiba's mastery of a number of martial arts and an integration of Zen and Buddhist thought combined with the Japanese concept of **bushido,** the spirit of samurai chivalry, dedication, and loyalty. The Japanese characters for *bushido* are often translated "stopping the spear"—studying the processes of making war to polish oneself and, paradoxically, to study acts of war to stop war and achieve the balance of harmony (Nitobe, 1905).

Ueshiba practiced aikido daily until his death in 1969 at the age of 86! The practice of aikido does not require great size, strength, or speed. It is often called the gentle martial art. "The central premise of Aikido is blending. Rather than compete with an attack, you blend, accommodate, control, and resolve it. Ai-Ki-Do, translates into English as, 'Harmony,' 'Spirit,' 'Path.' Aikido is not an art of fighting and violence, but an art of loving protection—a way to reconcile the world, a path with sincerity and heart" (Dobson, 1980, p. 52).

Aikido involves no contests or tournaments because they promote competition, which is directly contrary to its underlying philosophy. Rather, aikido students test for levels of proficiency. The tests are situations during which the student is given a chance to demonstrate proficiency in using techniques at various levels of development—beginner to third-degree black belt. Higher degrees through seventh-degree black belt and up are awarded for service, proficiency, leadership, and professionalism.

Specific techniques in aikido are studied and practiced against a variety of potential attacks. The focus of these techniques is to blend with the attacker's energy and utilize it to bring the attacker under control or to project the attacker away in such a way that neither party is harmed. Although the potential for harm does exist within most aikido techniques (otherwise it would not be an effective martial art), the preferred choice is to use minimal force to achieve a harmonious resolution—a position in which the attacker is under control, the attack is stopped, and both people are physically safe. The general purpose of studying aikido is "to promote a deeper understanding and appreciation of the perfection of nature's balance, and to bring humanity back in harmony [with nature]" (Saotome, 1985, p. 11). At its higher levels, aikido is an "effective discipline for the development, integration, and utilization of all man's powers, physical, and mental" (Westbrook & Ratti, 1988, p. 17).

Aikido recently has been used as a basis for understanding conflict and for specifying how to manage it. Several authors have transferred its principles from the dojo mat to everyday life. Koichi Tohei, a senior student of aikido's founder, was an early author to apply aikido principles in common contexts. In his book *Aikido in Daily Life,* he provides principles for living a stress-free (conflict-free) life. Terry Dobson, who was the only American to live with students of the aikido founder and a fifth-degree black belt in aikido, first applied aikido principles to verbal conflict in a book entitled *Giving in to Get Your Way.* The book was written at a time when aikido was first being brought to this country; as such, there is no reference to aikido in the title. Thomas Crum, a fifth-degree black belt in aikido, has offered the book *The Magic of Conflict,* in which he uses principles from conflict to elaborate both the nature of conflict and general conflict management principles, concepts, and techniques. Crum also has written several manuals for elementary teachers and students using aikido principles for conflict management. Another student of aikido, Donna Markova, uses principles she learned in aikido to discuss ways of managing conflict in *The Art of the Possible.* Richard Heckler, a fifth-degree black belt in aikido, has written or edited a number of books in which he and other authors provide examples of applying aikido principles to everyday life, including handling conflict, particularly his book *The Anatomy of Change.* In the June/July 1996 issue of *Aikido Today Magazine,* all of the major articles are devoted to using principles of aikido to address conflict in common contexts.

Managing conflict, as presented in this book, will be based on the basic aikido principles of blending, joining, and connecting with a person's energy, utilizing that energy to unbalance and then to move toward harmony. An example from a common occurrence in a classroom will illustrate an application of aikido principles to a potential verbal conflict.

Several students sitting in the back of the room have been whispering and talking rather than paying attention to Ms. Talbert's presentation or participating in the class discussion. The students' disregard for the teaching is disruptive to Ms. Talbert and students in the classroom. If Ms. Talbert asks the students to be quiet and to stop disrupting the classroom (an attempt to eliminate conflict), the potential arises for increasing the conflict. Even though Ms. Talbert might nicely ask the students to be quiet, she would draw the attention of the entire class to the students in question. Usually, when students behave in this way, they respond by defending themselves to save face among their peers. Frequently, they argue back that "They weren't doing anything." This student response often prompts teachers to explain what was observed. This teacher reaction may escalate the conflict until the teacher asks the students involved to leave the classroom or to move to different desks in an attempt to control the disruption.

Applying the aikido principle of accepting, blending, and using the student's energy could produce a different result. Ms. Talbert could use the student's energy and lead in a positive direction. The situation might unfold as follows:

Ms. Talbert: I'm sorry, Steve. I didn't hear what you wanted to say.

At this point Steve shakes his head no and looks down at his desk. Ms. Talbert says, "Thanks," and returns to her presentation. Her reaction to Steve's disruptive behavior accepts it as part of the presentation and discussion. Her response uses Steve's behavior/energy and focuses it in a new direction. Steve, of course, has nothing to contribute to the discussion and declines but now knows that Ms. Talbert has singled him out and will be watching. Harmony has been restored without Steve loosing serious face among his peers. In addition, there has been minimal interruption of the presentation and discussion. This basic aikido principle of accepting and blending will be applied in a variety of ways through a number of techniques for managing conflict and moving toward restoring the balance of harmony.

ORGANIZATION OF THE BOOK

Our intention in this book is to provide principles and concepts for understanding sources of conflict and how it is created and maintained and to describe practical techniques and programs for managing conflict in a productive way to restore harmony. In Chapter 2, we present a model for examining interpersonal relationships—contracts. The violation of contracts is the basis for many conflicts. Chapter 3 contains a discussion of the natural communicative processes that people use to create and maintain conflicts. In Chapter 4 is an examination of some of the naturally occurring processes that lead students to create conflicts in school. You will be introduced to 10 ways of dealing with conflict in Chapter 5, ending with the way that best exemplifies the basic principles of aikido, including accepting, blending, joining, unbalancing, and utilizing the energy in conflicts—the confluent response. A more detailed discussion of the confluent response is presented in Chapter 6. One of the recent developments in counseling psychology is solution-oriented counseling. The focus in solution-focused counseling is on finding and creating solutions to problems rather than on discovering and eliminating causes of problems. These approaches have many things in common with the basic aikido principles used in this book. In Chapter 7 you will be introduced to the application of some of the solution-oriented counseling principles applied to managing conflict to restore harmony. Conflicts occur in a variety of ways, and one is through multiple attacks—one person being attacked by several others. Several forms of multiple attacks will be described in Chapter 8 along with strategies for dealing with them. Although conflict is natural, ways of managing student classroom behaviors can help prevent the occurrence of conflicts. A number of classroom management techniques to prevent conflicts are described in Chapter 9. A recent development to managing conflicts in schools is mediation programs, described in Chapter 10. In addition, in Chapter 11 are a discussion and outline for developing a peer mediation program in which students act as mediators for their fellow students. Although the majority of this book focuses on managing conflicts using aikido principles, those same principles can be used in a positive way. In Chapter 12, you will find a discussion of a number of principles for preventing conflicts in classrooms.

SUMMARY

Conflict is natural. It occurs in the natural order of life and is part of the human condition. Differences in gender, ethnic heritage, age, physical size, social economic class, status, and role all provide potential for conflict between or among people. From our perspective, the goal of teachers should be to understand conflict and to manage the situation in a way that results in learning and the restoration and/or maintenance of harmony. The underlying principle of accepting, blending, joining, and using energy from the Japanese martial art aikido has been introduced as a basic foundation for dealing with conflicts.

REFERENCES

Aikido Today Magazine. (June/July 1996).

Batra, R. (1987). *The great depression of 1990*. New York: Simon & Schuster.

Crum, T. F. (1987). *The magic of conflict*. New York: Simon & Schuster.

Dobson. T. (1980). *When push comes to shove: Handling problem people*. Burlington, VT: Workshop Materials.

Fuller, J. R. (1988). Martial arts and psychological health. *British Journal of Medical Psychology, 61,* 317–328.

Hall, E. T. (1981). *Beyond culture*. New York: Doubleday.

Heckler, R. S. (1993). *The anatomy of change*. Berkeley, CA: North Atlantic Books.

Markova, D. (1991). *The art of the possible*. Emeryville, CA: Conari.

Nitobe, I. (1905). *Bushido, the soul of Japan*. New York: Putnam's, Knickerbocker.

Saotome, M. (1985). *Aikido and the harmony of nature*. Boulogne, France: SEDIREP.

Strauss, W., & Howe, N. (1991). *Generations*. New York: Morrow.

Tannen, D. (1990). *You just don't understand*. New York: Morrow.

Tohei, K. (1966). *Aikido in daily life*. Tokyo: Komiyama.

Westbrook, A., & Ratti, O. (1988). *Aikido and the dynamic sphere*. Rutland, VA: Tuttle.

CHAPTER 2

Roles, Contracts, and Conflict

A primary source of conflict in schools stems from role differences and expectations concerning those roles. Frequently, people's activities within groups are organized in terms of roles. Roles are related to the labels used to highlight aspects of lives within a cultural context. The process of growing up and living within a culture can be examined as a series of roles assigned or assumed in certain situations. We use labels such as parent, teacher, spouse, child, or grandparent to describe specific positions within specific social contexts. These roles are ways of organizing our behavior and thinking or standardizing our perceptions about people.

We occupy various roles concurrently. Jim, one of the authors, for example, occupies at this time major roles of eldest son, brother, spouse, father, uncle, professor, colleague, friend, and board of directors member. During any day, Jim also may occupy the roles of car driver, cook, customer, golfer, aikido student, pedestrian, or house cleaner. These roles are assumed or assigned within contexts. For example, in contexts such as an extended family Thanksgiving dinner, Jim will play a number of roles—son, spouse, father, or uncle—depending on the focus of the conversation. While at work, the university context, Jim will be in the roles of professor and colleague. In the context of schools, the terms *principal, teacher,* and *student* automatically create expectations about ways that people in those roles are supposed to behave. Expectations for roles within schools will vary by the level of the school (elementary to high school), area of the country, size of the school, and rural versus urban setting. Context and culture are very similar. For example, when a student is within a classroom, the expectation is that the student will pay attention to the teacher and engage in learning activities. This is part of the **culture** within schools.

CONTRACTS

The concept of culture has been difficult to define because its influence is so pervasive. Being within a cultural context is similar to being a fish in water. While in the water, the fish usually is not aware of the water; only when removed from the water does the fish become aware of it. It is similar with culture. While we are immersed in a cultural context, we usually are not aware of it. Only when we are transposed to a different culture or confronted with our present culture do we become aware of it. In discussing counseling, Larson (1982) suggests that each person has three identities: an individual identity, a group identity, and a universal identity.

> If viewed only in the context of his or her universality, . . . a person loses his or her individuality; if viewed only in the context of his or her individuality, the person loses a sense of connectedness with humanity; if viewed only in the context of group membership, an individual is stereotyped. The delicate task in counseling is to integrate all three views when working with clients. (p. 844)

Race and culture influence the way we think about ourselves and others—our roles. Although we recognize the individual nuances of both, we believe that a discussion of race and culture together has greater explanatory power. We base our discussion on the works of a number of authors (Brammer, 1993; Corey & Corey, 1993; Gorden, 1992; Hutchins & Cole, 1992; Okun, 1992) but believe that Edward T. Hall (1981) has made a particularly significant contribution in this area.

Hall (1981), in his book *Beyond Culture,* suggests that "humans are tied to each other by hierarchies of rhythms that are **culture-specific** and expressed through language and body movement" (p. 74). He offers that cultures can be divided into two classes: **high-context** cultures and **low-context** cultures. In discussing these cultural types, Hall makes it clear that people from the two contexts experience distinct differences in how they perceive and interpret life's events and roles. As one moves from the low to the high side of the scale, awareness of the selective screen that one places between oneself and the outside world increases. A person from a high-context culture will be *very* aware of how messages are transmitted within role contexts. In contrast, a person from a low-context culture will be less aware of the manner and more aware of the message being transmitted within role contexts. Hall suggests that the "level of context determines everything about the nature of communication and is the foundation on which all subsequent behavior rests" (p. 92). Specifically, a "high-context (HC) communication or message is one in which most of the information is either in the physical context or internalized in the person, while very little is in the coded, explicit, transmitted part of the message. A low-context (LC) communication is just the opposite, i.e., the mass of the information is vested in the explicit code" (p. 91).

When Hall's postulates are applied to specific cultural contexts, we can determine that the German, Swiss, and Scandinavian cultures, for instance, are very low-context cultures, whereas Chinese, Korean, Japanese, and most African cultures are high-context cultures. A majority of the American culture is considered to be at the low end of the continuum between low- and high-context cultures, whereas the Native American culture is at the high end.

From an applied perspective, Hall's work leads us to realize that people from different cultures have fundamentally different ways of screening information, processing inputs, and communicating with others. People from high-context cultures are highly dependent on the context of the interaction. They usually are more socially oriented and pay attention to facial expressions and body language. Indirect forms of communication are important in their communication (e.g., elaborate stories, parables). By contrast, people from low-context cultures focus on the content of the spoken message. They use observations of facial expressions and body language to augment what they understand from the spoken message but are less likely to use facial expressions or body language as the **primary** message transmitter. Unlike their high-context counterparts, people from low-context cultures prefer direct, language-specific communication.

It is important that teachers become aware of basic differences in culture-based communicative styles. Communication styles affect expectations attached to various roles. In doing so, teachers also should be aware of their personal cultural learning and be open to the contextual preferences of their students. It is the teacher's responsibility to bridge the gap that may exist.

Axelson (1985) provides a useful definition of culture: "A cultural system is the process that a group of people have developed for satisfying needs, for solving problems, and for adjusting to both the external environment and to each other" (p. 5). This definition focuses on agreements, expectations, rules, and requirements within groups—racial, ethnic, and gender.

Efran, Lukens, and Lukens (1990) call these expectations contractual arrangements that solidify roles and cultural structures including relationships. **Contracts** are legal or binding agreements between or among people. They are either explicit or implicit. **Explicit contracts** usually are in the form of laws or written rules. **Implicit contracts** are the expectations that accompany roles within cultural contexts. When contracts, either explicit or implicit, are broken, legal, psychological, or physical consequences may occur. Legal consequences are dealt with in the judicial system. Psychological and physical consequences result in stress reactions. For example, when we are in the role of car driver, there are contractual rules about which side of the road to drive on, the right side in the United States and the left in Great Britain and Japan. When we are in the role of pedestrian, there are implicit contractual rules about which side of the walk to use (usually the right) and which door in a set of double doors is for entering and which door is for exiting. When people violate such implicit contracts, it causes confusion, annoyance, conflict, and sometimes injury, as when, for example, someone unexpectedly goes through the wrong door or drives on the wrong side of the road.

We even have contracts about contracts—what to do when an explicit or implicit rule or law is broken. When a person walks through the wrong door and bumps into someone, the contract about contracts specifies that she or he should apologize. When people do not fulfill the secondary contract, they are often labeled rude. When we hold a door open for someone, we expect them to say thank you, a contract about a contract. When people do not say thank you, they too are labeled rude. Such contracts are woven completely into every role of daily life and within cultural contexts. It is useful to describe the orchestrated patterns of roles in contractual terms rather than simply in terms of expectations, understandings, belief systems, or assumptive structures. The language of contracts conveys the active, urgent nature and consequences when these implicit or explicit contracts are broken (Efran et al., 1990).

Contracts place a virtual demand on behavior when a person is in a particular role. For example, in our larger U.S. culture, without speaking or asking for directions, people know to go to the end of the line at a store checkout; when they do not, they are reminded forcefully and vociferously by those waiting in line. These contracts form the basis for reciprocity in relationships. **Reciprocity** refers to the interactive effect in relationships; that is, what one person does has a direct effect on the type of response that the person will receive. When actions and interactions proceed normally, reciprocity is maintained—each person in the interaction has a positive experience. When reciprocity is not maintained, conflict occurs.

Contracts are even made with oneself. We often make contracts with ourselves or between the various roles we hold. The kind of promises and resolutions that we might make on New Year's Day are examples of self-directed contracts: "I'm going to start an exercise program and get in shape!"; "I'm going to lose 20 pounds by spring!";

"I'm not going to yell at the kids anymore!" Contracts that are broken or left incomplete create conflict and take their toll on relationships as well as on the psychological and physical health of the person breaking the contract or leaving it unfilled.

Efran et al. (1990) suggest:

> Every contractual transgression is a personal and communal liability [conflict]. Even transgressions [conflicts] that others agree to overlook or politely excuse as unimportant extract a price—they accumulate and gradually erode the quality of life. This is the complaint of many city-dwellers who find that nobody seems to give a damn—neither salesclerks, city workers, government officials, repair people, contractors, landlords, nor pet owners. In the conversation of living, complete agreements are sources of self-satisfaction, but incomplete or broken agreements shackle self-esteem and drain vitality. . . . Because broken agreements [conflicts] simultaneously weaken the social fabric and tarnish self-image, a good rule of thumb in life . . . is to keep every agreement you make. (p. 117)

Making and breaking contracts is the essence of how self-concept, self-esteem, and self-efficacy are built, maintained, and damaged. People who fulfill their contracts, explicit or implicit, feel good about themselves and create a strong sense of self-esteem. Fulfilling contracts also leads to a stronger sense of self-concept as someone who can walk their talk. When people walk their talk, a stronger sense of self-efficacy is developed. The positive effects of fulfilling contracts or the negative effects of breaking them is especially true for the contracts that people make with themselves or those close to them. Because meaning is developed primarily around language (our words), those who keep their word (i.e., fulfill their contracts) will have a more positive self-concept, higher self-esteem, and a greater sense of self-efficacy. Further, because the mind and body are so closely connected, breaking contracts also leaves some negative physical residual—stress. People can literally make themselves weaker and even susceptible to disease by continually breaking their contracts with themselves and/or others.

The primary contract that people make with others is the simple reciprocal contract: "If I do something for you, you should do something in return for me." This form of contract is the basis of much of people's behavior until higher forms of moral development occur. People use this model to make friends and develop and maintain relationships. If we give of ourselves to others, there is a contract that the others ought to return the favor or at least acknowledge the giving. If they do not, conflict occurs. The implicit contract is broken, and relationships are often terminated or damaged. This simple "purchase-of-service" model is the basis of some abuse and misunderstanding, as, for example, in the case of the person who tries to buy friends by giving others gifts. The expectation is "If I give you a gift, you should be my friend."

People develop reciprocal contracts and use them to evaluate their responses to significant others in their lives. The form of the contract does not matter unless the person is psychotic or psychopathic. Psychotic or psychopathic people often develop contracts that are harmful to themselves or others. When given the three themes of "What did a significant person do for me?" "What did I do for them?" and "What problems did I cause them?" most people will be able to analyze their own failings in fulfilling their contracts. Answering such questions focuses on the person's own standards, not necessarily those imposed by others. This analysis of failed and broken contracts can become a strong motivator for changing future behavior.

In our language, contracts often are stated as rules through the use of words such as *have to, should, ought, must,* and *can't*. For example, "You *have to* take other people's feelings into account!" is the statement of an implicit contract that the speaker uses to make decisions about how to treat others. We learn such contract statements over time from significant others and from our interactions with others whom we respect. Teachers can help students identify their contracts by listening carefully for statements that contain such contractual words. The word *can't* most often is a negative form of contract that specifies the speaker's perceived or self-imposed limitations. Often, students state their contracts without specifying consequences of breaking them. Teachers can help students make consequences explicit by asking questions similar to "What will happen if you don't . . . ?" or, in the case of the negative contracts with *can't,* "What prevents you from . . . ?" Consider the following example:

TEACHER: What will happen if you don't take other people's feelings into account?

A typical student response might be:

SARAH: Well, they won't like you.

We find that a simple listening response of repeating the two student statements together makes the contract explicit and allows the student to examine it in its full meaning.

T: You have to control your behavior to make people feel good so that they can like you.

SARAH: It sounds kind of silly when you put it that way!

Notice that the teacher did not put it any way other than what the student had said. When confronted with their own contracts, people often see the limitations of them.

Now consider an example of negative contracts:

SARAH: I can't drop chemistry.

T: What prevents you?

SARAH: My parents will be really disappointed if I do.

T: So your parents' possible reactions keep you from making a decision.

SARAH: Yeah! My parents want me to be a doctor, and I want to be an engineer.

T: What do you want to do about these differences in your wants and those of your parents?

Some of students' language is a direct key to contracts that they use to govern their lives.

The concept of contracts within specific cultural groups has important implications in schools. Teachers working with students from cultures different than their own must pay special attention to their personal biases. In addition, they must become familiar with roles and contracts particular to students' racial or ethnic groups. Teachers also can help students identify ways in which contracts affect their lives (e.g., implicit and explicit contracts that exist for students about studying, working, and respecting others). Contracts associated with being in any role vary from situation to situation. Students may have different explicit contracts about behavior for each interpersonal interaction. Teachers can help students analyze how breaking these contracts affects their feelings of self-worth and self-efficacy. Also, teachers can help students understand how their own promises to self, friends, and others are really contracts that, when broken, can take their toll on psychological and physical health as well as relationships. Psychological health, as described earlier, revolves around ways of thinking about oneself (self-concept), feeling about oneself (self-esteem), and using power to affect one's environment (self-efficacy).

EXPLICIT CONTRACTS

Schools have their idiosyncratic set of explicit contracts—student conduct rules. These rules often include the following:

- Do not run in the halls.
- No smoking on school grounds.
- Permission slips are required to be in the hall during class time.
- Tardy or absence slips are needed if you are late for school or a class.
- Remain in your seat and participate meaningfully during class.
- Do not throw food in the cafeteria.

Teachers frequently develop their own explicit contracts for behavior within their classrooms in addition to those of the school. The requirements and levels of performance for achieving certain grades within each class are other forms of explicit contracts. Students usually are instructed in such rules and explicit contracts during orientations. When students break these explicit contracts, conflict is created. Students usually are punished in some way for breaking explicit contracts—they are sent to the principal's or dean of discipline's office, they are sent home or expelled for flagrant violations, notes are mailed to parents, or a parent-teacher conference is arranged.

IMPLICIT CONTRACTS

Implicit rules vary among schools. The variance in implicit rules will depend on community and cultural differences. Schools in rural communities may have different explicit and implicit contracts than those in large inner-city schools. However, we think universal implicit contracts exist in most schools because of the larger American culture. For example:

- Walk on the right.
- Use the doors on the right.
- Do not steal others' belongings.
- Respect school property.
- Teachers are in school to teach.
- Students should do their homework.
- Respect your elders.

When students or teachers break explicit and implicit contracts, the usual psychological and physical toll and potential effects on self-concepts and self-esteem result. In addition, when contracts are broken, the potential for conflict arises. A student running down the hall, breaking an explicit contract, may bump into fellow students and knock them down. The offended students may shove back, resulting in a prolonged confrontation. A student who breaks the implicit contract of showing teachers respect may initiate a loud argument that disrupts the class and leads to the student being sent to the principal's office. You likely can think of other examples from your own experience.

SUMMARY

Roles and the implicit and explicit contracts accompanying them are the fiber that holds society together. They also define differences among people and cultures. When people break contracts, the potential for conflict and psychological and physical stress emerges. This is true even for contracts with oneself. Understanding, accepting, and acting in accordance with contracts are the basis for restoring and maintaining harmony within ourselves and with one another.

REFERENCES

Axelson, J. A. (1985). *Counseling and development in a multicultural society.* Pacific Grove, CA: Brooks/Cole.

Brammer, L. M. (1993). *The helping relationship* (5th ed.). Boston: Allyn & Bacon.

Corey, M. S., & Corey, G. (1993). *Becoming a helper* (2nd ed.). Pacific Grove, CA: Brooks/Cole.

Efran, J. S., Lukens, M. D., & Lukens, R. J. (1990). *Language structure and change.* New York: Norton.

Gorden, R. (1992). *Basic interviewing skills.* Itasca, IL: Peacock.

Hall, E. T. (1981). *Beyond culture.* New York: Doubleday.

Hutchins, D. E., & Cole, C. G. (1992). *Helping relationships and strategies* (2nd ed.). Pacific Grove, CA: Brooks/Cole.

Larson, P. C. (1982). Counseling special populations. *Professional Psychology, 13,* 843–858.

Okun, B. F. (1992). *Effective helping: Interviewing and counseling techniques* (4th ed.). Pacific Grove, CA: Brooks/Cole.

CHAPTER 3

How We Create and Maintain Conflict

In the example presented in Chapter 1, a teacher, one vocal and emotional parent, and other parents exhibited mixed feelings. All came together in a teacher's classroom. Imagine yourself in that situation.

It is Parents' Night at school in early October. A sixth-grade teacher, Mr. Rich, begins to address a room full of parents, when a parent stands up and begins to criticize him because of his teaching style and classroom organization. It is obvious that the parent is very upset. The parent's criticism is about the modern methods that Mr. Rich has been using. The parent wants Mr. Rich to return to the basics and stop all the fancy stuff.

> PARENT: Mr. Rich, I don't think what you are doing with all this open classroom stuff is going to teach my son or other people's kids the basics they need to succeed in school. What is this all about, that students help set their own goals? Whatever happened to the good old-fashioned reading, writing, and arithmetic?

By noticing the head nods of other parents, Mr. Rich realizes that some parents share similar feelings. Other parents remain silent. Still others seem embarrassed by this parent's outburst.

When enmeshed in a conflict situation such as this one, typically it is difficult to control your emotional reactions. It also is difficult to exercise authority inherent in your role as a teacher. The fact that you are in your classroom adds another dimension. That is, in this environment, usually you are in control. In this situation, you may not feel that you are. You do have one advantage, however. You know what you feel and what you perceive to be occurring. Your task is to control your emotions, gain a clearer understanding of your adversary, and use your position and skills to move toward a harmonious management of the conflict. To do this, you must be aware of specifics that affect your perceptions. For instance, you must be aware of the reactions of the remaining parents. There also are the potential responses of your colleagues and your administrator to how you handle the situation. If you are going to share this experience with a loved one later, then this likelihood also will influence your response. All of these contextual dimensions affect how you respond to the conflict raised by one parent in your classroom.

By taking time to assess the situation, you can become a participant observer; that is, while participating in the interaction, you also can observe the interaction. Assuming a participant-observer role is a state of mind requiring you to put your ego aside so that you can focus your attention simultaneously on those around you as well as on your own internal reactions. It is similar to carrying on running commentary with yourself about what you are experiencing while you are continuing to participate in the interaction. From this perspective, you will be able to observe the situation and hypothesize the consequences of any action. This perspective will help you control your emotions and maximize your options. Finally, being a participant observer will provide a perspective from which you will be able to choose a strategy to manage the conflict in a constructive manner that increases the possibility that harmony will be restored.

Teachers frequently are expected to mediate conflict situations. Even when not directly attacked verbally or physically, teachers are challenged to assess situations and mediate between others without imposing their personal perceptions and feelings. The potential difficulty inherent in such situations is the possibility of being forced out of a participant-observer role and elevated into the middle of the conflict. Even though you may attempt to remain a participant observer, prior experiences with the participants establishes you as being integral to the conflict. Your prior experiences will affect others' openness and responsiveness to your efforts to mediate.

We assume that you will be involved in conflict situations, either directly or indirectly. Therefore, we believe that it is necessary and useful to assess the dynamics surrounding conflict. More specifically, we believe that attending to relationships is most useful. The emotional states of students and teachers need to be considered. You must consider the context of interactions. Finally, it is important to understand the verbal nature of conflict. Each of these elements will be discussed in this chapter.

ELEMENTS IN THE PROCESS

Students, teachers, parents, administrators, or pupil personnel service workers are the primary parties in school conflicts. Each of these parties may need to alter their behavior and attitudes for conflicts to be meaningfully managed and balance or harmony restored. Mediators—including students' peers, faculty, administrators, student personnel workers, parents, and others in the community who are affected by or contribute to the conflict and its management—are secondary parties.

In the example of a parent confronting a teacher on Parents' Night, the primary people are the teacher and the verbally attacking parent. Other parents in the room, their children, and the building administrator are secondary parties. To the extent that a curriculum has been adopted by a department, one's colleagues also become secondary parties.

A second level that can be examined is the context in which interaction takes place. Returning to the original example, the classroom is the primary context. A primary context can be any place in and around the school. The primary context becomes significant in dealing with conflict because the rules and the status of the parties change from classroom, hallway, playground, school grounds, or the principal's or counselor's office. In the Parents' Night example, the school building with its rules and regulations becomes the secondary context and the home and possibly the community become the third context level. In dealing with conflict, knowing whether an individual is a primary or secondary party and, further, knowing contextual rules are all important for becoming an effective agent in restoring harmony.

SOURCES OF CONFLICT

As mentioned earlier, conflict occurs because of naturally occurring differences in gender, age, physical size, and social-economic status. All of these contribute to the formation of student and faculty groups or cliques that often are polarized around real or imagined differences.

Gender

Neimeyer and Metzler (1987) found that males and females differ in how they organize experiences and information. Males emphasize differences, and females emphasize commonalities. Among female students there is little separation, if any, between primary and secondary parties when peer conflict arises. By contrast, males tend to be less loyal, look out for themselves, and are less concerned with peers in individual conflicts *unless* conflict occurs between two different, personally important, identifiable groups.

Gottfredson (1981) explains how gender differences suggested by Neimeyer and Metzler are formed and how they influence decisions. Her observations of children's development led her to hypothesize that the seemingly higher social status of males is due in large part to children seeing adult males as bigger, stronger, and more powerful than females. She suggests that based on this early perception, males are likely to be assertive and females more likely to be passive—as a general rule. By inference, in conflict situations, males are more likely to strike out assertively to maintain their independence, whereas females are more likely to take a passive approach or work actively toward interpersonal resolution.

Adlerian psychology offers a slightly different perspective. Adler's (1930) research emphasizes the strong impact of childhood experiences. In Adlerian psychology, the father is considered to be the most potent influence on the male child's formation of values. By contrast, the mother is the most potent influence on a female child. From an Adlerian perspective, parental influence on value formation is established before age eight and is reinforced in adolescence through visual recollections. One result of role definition, as presented in Adlerian psychology, is that females are more likely to see themselves through the eyes of others, thus being more responsive to social pressure. Males are enculturated to be less socially attuned and less responsive to social pressure.

Society is in a time of values transition. We are experiencing major change in social roles of males and females. Some households fit a traditional Adlerian model. Other households encourage children of both genders to cue into both parents' values. Still other households may be between these two extremes. An increasing number of children are raised in single-parent homes. The consequence of this values transition and differences among families have profoundly affected all children but seem to have had a greater impact on females. That is, female children seem to have heightened confusion about what constitutes appropriate values for themselves.

We realize that these are gender generalizations. However, teacher-mediators might benefit from using these generalizations as working hypotheses. In doing so, they are cautioned to maintain sensitivity to the possibility of differences while actively *reading* individuals or groups.

VERBAL CONFLICTS

Although conflicts can take many forms, the majority of conflicts in schools are verbal conflicts. It is important to understand how conflicts are created and maintained to understand how to avoid them. When implicit or explicit contracts are broken, others may come to the aid of involved individuals. The people involved may try to resolve the conflict, but their actions may fuel the flames of further conflict. On the following pages, we note ways that people attempt to manage conflicts. In some cases, their efforts maintain or increase the conflict. Keep in mind that the communicative responses outlined here may not be problematic in nonconflict situations. Also, remember that the tone of voice and nonverbal behavior accompanying the examples will have an effect on potential responses. As you read the examples, imagine an appropriate negative tone of voice, facial expression, or gesture.

Imposing Contracts

Imposing contracts take the communicative form of orders or commands. These usually are expressed in an imperative form.

"You Have to. . . . "

SANDRA: *[angrily]* You have to give that back!

LISA: *[defiantly]* Yeah, make me!

"You Will. . . . "

TEACHER: *[exasperated]* You will stop talking, now!

PAT: *[whiny]* How come you never tell Jane that?

"Don't You Think . . . ?"

TEACHER: *[sarcastically]* Don't you think that's enough, Pat?

PAT: *[sarcastically]* No, I'm not finished!

"You Can't. . . . "

KRIS: *[threateningly]* You can't sit here!

GAIL: *[defiantly]* Yeah, who's going to stop me?

"Stay in Your Seat!"

TEACHER: *[frustrated]* Sit down and stay in your seat!

ELIZABETH: *[whiny]* I was just going to sharpen my pencil. How am I supposed to do my work?

These forms of communication often produce fear and/or active resistance. They are an invitation to testing and defiance. They also promote rebellious behavior and possible retaliation. All of these possibilities either maintain or intensify conflict.

Warnings and Threats

Warnings and threats can both produce and/or maintain conflict.

"If You Don't . . . , Then. . . . "

TEACHER: *[angrily]* If you don't start working with your child, then she will flunk this course!

PARENT: *[angrily]* Why don't you teach better?

"You Had Better . . . , or Else. . . . "

TEACHER: *[exasperated]* You had better sit down, or else you're going to the principal's office.

RALPH: *[angrily]* Yeah? Well, then at least I'd be out of this class!

"Try That Again and I'll. . . . "

SUSIE: *[angrily]* Try that again and I'll tell Mrs. Phillips!

PAULINE: *[challenging]* Oh, yeah! Such a crybaby!

"Don't You Dare . . . or I'll. . . . "

TEACHER: *[angrily]* Don't you dare go to the principal about this, or I'll give you more homework than you can handle!

BRUCE: *[defiantly]* Yeah? Well, we'll see about that!

"You Do That One More Time and I'll. . . . "

STEVE: *[angrily]* You do that one more time and I'll knock you silly!

KEVIN: *[defiantly]* You try that and I'll punch your lights out!

Warnings and threats are aimed at producing fear and submission. These approaches usually are attempts to stop conflict. However, they usually produce the opposite. Warnings and threats tend to invite testing the threatened consequences and usually cause resentment, anger, and rebellion—the very things that maintain or intensify conflict.

Moralizing and Preaching

Moralizing and preaching are similar to imposing contracts on others. They differ linguistically in the use of words such as *should, ought, can't, have to,* and *yet.* These words may imply a moral obligation to follow what is stated.

"You Should. . . . "

TEACHER: *[exasperated]* Get your feet off that desk. You should be more respectful of school property!

LOUIS: *[defiantly]* Why are you on my case? Everybody does it!

"You Ought to. . . . "

PARENT: *[angrily]* You ought to have better discipline here, then my son wouldn't be harassed by those other students!

PRINCIPAL: *[defensively]* We do our best! Your son needs to learn to avoid those situations.

"You Have to. . . . "

TEACHER: *[angrily]* You have to stop letting those students switch classes. I'm having trouble keeping track of what's going on!

VICE PRINCIPAL: *[defensively]* Get your act together and the students wouldn't want to switch classes!

"You Can't. . . . "

PRINCIPAL: *[angrily]* You can't keep grading students so low in your classes. Parents are getting upset!

TEACHER: *[defensively]* Are telling me how to assign grades in my class?

"Have You . . . Yet?"

TEACHER: *[exasperated]* Have you gotten that project done yet?

DIANE: *[whiny]* I'm working on it. Get off my back!

Moralizing and preaching usually are used in an attempt to produce a sense of obligation, guilt, or responsibility, which people often resist. This produces more conflict. When people are moralized or preached to, they most often resist and defend themselves or their position and conflict is increased. Finally, moralizing and preaching often communicate a lack of trust in the person's sense of responsibility.

Giving Advice and Suggesting Solutions

Giving advice or suggesting solutions may be appropriate in helping situations but not in conflict situations. In some ways giving advice and suggesting solutions can sound like moralizing and preaching.

"What I Would Do Is. . . . "

TEACHER: What I'd do is talk to your parents about that.

LEO: I couldn't do that! My parents think I'm doing just fine.

"Why Don't You . . . ?"

TEACHER: Why don't you talk this over with your counselor?

MILLIE: *[defensively]* I couldn't do that—I'd be too embarrassed!

"I Want You to Try. . . . "

TEACHER: *[angrily]* Gail! I want you to try to stay in your seat!

GAIL: *[whiny]* I wasn't doing anything. Pat took my pencil!

"I Think What You Should Do Is. . . . "

PRINCIPAL: *[impatiently]* I think what you should do is to establish stricter conduct rules in your class!

TEACHER: *[defensively]* What do you mean? What I need is more support from the administration around here!

"You Need to. . . . "

TEACHER: *[impatiently]* If you want your daughter to do better in this class, you need to make sure she does her homework!

PARENT: *[angrily]* It's not my job to teach my kids! That's your job!

Giving advice and offering solutions may imply that the other person cannot solve his or her own problem and, in a conflict situation, implies that he or she is responsible for the conflict. Since a solution has been offered, it prevents the person from exploring or trying other alternatives. Responses of this nature often produce resistance and continued argument—an intensification of the conflict.

Arguing and Persuading

Arguing and persuading automatically maintains or increases conflict. Typical types of arguing or persuading are as follows.

"Here Is Why You're Wrong"

TEACHER: *[exasperated]* You really don't know what you're talking about. Here's why you're wrong. That student directly challenged me by calling me _____, and that's when I sent him to your office!

ASSISTANT PRINCIPAL: *[defensively]* I had to deal with the situation immediately! I didn't have time to gather all the facts!

"The Fact(s) Is (Are)...."

TEACHER: *[angrily]* The fact is you're totally wrong! I didn't tell the students that at all!

PRINCIPAL: *[angrily]* I've got three parents telling me that their children said you said that in their classes!

"Yes, but...."

PRINCIPAL: *[calmly]* We have been getting a lot of students from your classes being sent to the office.

TEACHER: *[defensively]* Yes, but look at all the bad students you put in my class!

"Well, You Did(n't)...."

PRINCIPAL: *[exasperated]* Well, you didn't tell us why you sent her down to the office!

TEACHER: *[exasperated]* Where is your support? She was mouthing off in class and disrupting things. I don't have time to write a report!

"What Do You Mean I...?"

TEACHER: *[angrily]* What do you mean I'm out to get your son?

PARENT: *[angrily]* You keep picking on him!

Arguing and persuading can produce counterarguments and resistance, which maintains or increases conflict. Arguing and persuading can turn off people and interfere with their ability to hear what is being said. They may feel put down and often will attempt to redeem themselves, continuing or intensifying the conflict.

Judging, Criticizing, and Blaming

Judging, criticizing, and blaming usually produce defensive behavior in others. This continues or intensifies conflict.

"You Aren't Thinking Maturely"

TEACHER: *[exasperated]* You can't keep challenging everything everybody says. You aren't thinking maturely!

WALDO: *[defiantly]* You keep telling us to question everything!

"You're Lazy!"

TEACHER: *[exasperated]* You're just lazy!

KEESHA: *[defiantly]* Oh, yeah! You just keep piling on the homework!

"You Don't Know What You're Doing!"

PRINCIPAL: *[impatiently]* You don't seem to know what you're doing! You send more students to the office than any other teacher!

TEACHER: *[defiantly]* It's not my fault! The students and their parents in my classes don't seem to care about learning anything!

"You're Stupid!"

TWILA: *[challenging]* You're stupid! You don't even know what we are talking about!

TODD: *[defensively]* I do too!

"You Don't Know What You're Talking About!"

PRINCIPAL: *[exasperated]* We've been getting a lot of complaints about your teaching lately.

TEACHER: *[defiantly]* You don't know what you're talking about! Come down to my classroom sometime and see what is going on!

When people make judging, criticizing, or blaming statements, they imply that the other person is incompetent, stupid, or has poor judgment. Judging, criticizing, and blaming statements stop effective communication. Statements of this type increase conflict and resentful feelings that lead to future conflict.

Praising and Agreeing

Praising and agreeing can be a put-down. In conflict situations, when people agree or praise particular behavior, it usually is done to diminish the other person—a put-down. The put-down can be heard in the speaker's tone of voice.

"Well, You Must Know It All"

TEACHER: *[sarcastically, responding to a advice from another teacher]* You must know all about how to run a classroom!

"I'm Sure You Have All the Answers"

TEACHER: *[sarcastically, responding to a wisecrack from a student]* I'm sure you have all the answers!

"You're Right!"

TEACHER: *[sarcastically, responding to critical advice from another teacher]* You're right! You're always right, aren't you?

"Why Don't You Tell Everybody What to Do?"

TEACHER: *[angrily responding to a critical parent]* Why don't you tell all of us teachers how to teach?

"You Seem to Know . . . Better than. . . . "

TEACHER: *[sarcastically, responding to a principal's critical comments]* You seem to know what's going on in my classroom better than I do!

Agreeing or praising put-downs often are patronizing and produce increased conflict because they are seen as manipulative and a form of sarcasm.

Ridiculing and Name-Calling

Ridiculing or name-calling is a form of verbal attack and, as such, will always produce conflict or exacerbate it.

"Crybaby!"

BRETT: *[whiny]* I'm going to tell Mrs. Smith!
BURT: *[sarcastically]* Crybaby!

BRETT: *[angrily]* I am not! You're a bully!

"OK, Smarty. . . . "

TEACHER: *[responding to a student's acting out behavior]* OK, smarty! Sit down!
FRANCIS: *[defiantly]* Why do I have to?

Any Kind of Epitaph Referring to Race or Gender

AARON: *[challenging]* Get your white fanny out of this area!
PAUL: *[defiantly]* Oh, yeah? Just who's going to make me?

"You're So Dumb!"

RALPH: *[responding to the advice of another student]* You're so dumb!
PAULETTE: *[angrily]* Yeah? And you seem to know it all!

"You're Such a Loser!"

FRED: *[sarcastically]* You're such a loser!
JUAN: *[challenging]* Yeah, and what makes you so great?

Name-calling or ridiculing is most often used as a verbal attempt to push an antagonist away. It usually has the opposite effect. The person ridiculed usually will fight back to defend her- or himself. Instead of reducing conflict, ridiculing usually exaggerates it.

Analyzing and Diagnosing

Analyzing or diagnosing is a process in which one person tries to handle conflict by examining the other person's behavior and/or attributing some form of motivation to it.

"You Don't Really Mean That!"

TEACHER: *[responding to a sarcastic student]* You didn't really mean that!
ADAM: *[whiny]* I did too! She's so dumb!

"You Just Want to Make Me Mad!"

TEACHER: *[responding to a sarcastic student]* You didn't really mean that! You just wanted to make me mad!
TONYA: *[angrily]* You're darn right! Get off my back!

"What's Wrong with You?"

TEACHER: *[exasperated]* What's wrong with you?

ANDREAS: *[angrily]* Nothing! Get off my back!

"You Just Hate [a Particular Racial or Gender Epitaph]!"

MIGUEL: *[angrily]* You just hate me because I'm Chicano!

LIAS: *[sarcastically]* Being Mexican has nothing to do with it! You're just stupid!

"You Just Like to Pick on People!"

JAMIE: *[defiantly]* You just like to pick on people!

PHIL: *[sarcastically]* Yeah! Especially losers like you!

Probing and Questioning

As with reassuring or sympathizing, outside people often try to mediate conflicts among others by probing and questioning the people involved. The mediator often asks questions such as these:

"Why Did You . . . ?"

TEACHER: Why did you do that?

JANE: *[defiantly]* Because he did it first!

"What Did You Do . . . ?"

TEACHER: *[demanding]* What did you do to her?

CARRIE: *[defiantly]* Nothing!

"Who Did . . . ?"

TEACHER: *[responding to a commotion in the classroom]* Who did that?

STUDENTS: *[Remain silent]*

TEACHER: *[again, demanding tone of voice]* Who did that?

BRUCE: *[wise-cracking]* It was the wind!

"How Did This Get Started?"

TEACHER: *[demanding]* How did this get started?

PATRICIA: *[defensively]* She started it!

"Who Started This?"

TEACHER: *[breaking up a scuffle in the hall]* Who started this?

JAN: *[defiantly]* He started it!

ROCIO: *[angrily]* I did not! He did!

Although probing and questioning are attempts to discover the source and responsibility of conflict, they frequently produce defensiveness in the people involved in the conflict. People intuitively know from personal experience that answering such questions usually requires some justification of themselves, and their answers usually produce criticism and blaming. An attempt by a teacher or fellow student to manage the situation by probing and questioning can maintain or exacerbate conflict rather than resolve it.

Diverting Attention, Withdrawing, and Using Sarcasm

When the person who initially breaks either an implicit or explicit contract that results in conflict attempts to divert attention, withdraw, or use sarcasm as a way of avoiding the conflict, she or he usually inflames it.

"Let's Talk about Something Else"

WILBUR: *[demanding]* What am I supposed to do?

TEACHER: *[disgusted]* Let's talk about something else!

WILBUR: *[frustrated]* Yeah, right! Thanks for the help!

Remaining Silent

KEVIN: *[sarcastically]* You're so stupid!

CHRIS: *[Remains silent]*

KEVIN: *[more sarcastically]* What's the matter, dummy—can't you even defend yourself?

Turning or Running Away

STACY: *[sarcastically]* Crybaby!

BILL: *[Turning away]*

STACY: *[more sarcastically]* Just hide your head in a hole!

"What's Your Problem?"

TEACHER: *[sarcastically]* What's your problem, Jack?

JACK: *[sarcastically]* It's not my problem! It's you who has the problem!

"What, You're Running the World?"

VIRGIL: *[sarcastically]* What, you're running the world?

SCOTT: *[sarcastically]* Yeah, you want to make something of it?

Diverting, sarcasm, and withdrawal imply that conflict is to be avoided rather than dealt with and managed. Also, they attribute responsibility for conflict to other people rather than the one who originally broke the implicit or explicit contract. Although used to manage conflict, diverting, sarcasm, or withdrawal usually maintain or exaggerate conflict.

The previous discussion has focused on ways verbal behavior maintains or produces conflict. Nonverbal behavior, considered to be 70% to 80% of all communication (Hamilton, Parker, & Smith, 1982), also contributes to maintaining or producing conflict. Nonverbal actions affect communication and further conflict in a number of ways.

NONVERBAL COMMUNICATION

Nonverbal communication relays messages. A person's attitudes, personality, and manner of dress can communicate an impression of attractiveness, acceptability, and group membership. Manner of dress communicates such things as social economic status, gang membership, or clique membership. It is a way of communicating belonging and differences. Sometimes, dress or appearance is a source of conflict (e.g., one gang versus another, the in-group versus the out-group). Teachers and students can benefit from understanding how such nonverbal communication contributes to conflict. This is especially important when dress and appearance codes are not honored. Some schools have specific explicit dress codes that, when violated, can cause conflict. For example, some schools prohibit students from wearing known gang colors to school as a way of attempting to control potential gang conflicts in the school.

Congruence between Verbal and Nonverbal Communication

Congruence between verbal and nonverbal behavior is extremely important. Consider the following example: When greeting an old friend you have not seen for some time, you might hug him and exclaim, "It's great to see you again!" In such a case, the verbal and nonverbal behavior is congruent. When communication is not congruent, the potential arises for misunderstanding, at least, or conflict, at worst. Keep in mind that nonverbal behavior includes not only actions and body postures but also tone of voice and inflection. Sometimes people are incongruent between verbal behavior and nonverbal behavior as a way of communicating sarcasm and negative judgments.

Physical Factors

Several nonverbal physical factors define differences that can lead to, or be used as, the basis for conflict.

- *Body build or size:* Several biases are based on body builds. In general, people who are tall, slim, and perceived to be good looking are more appreciated, sought out, and rewarded (Morris, 1977). People who are short and overweight usually are less sought after, less popular, and less rewarded. Such stereotypes often lead to communication and actions that are the basis for conflict.
- *Skin color:* The color of people's skin has been a strong stimulus for stereotypes and responses in our culture (Morris, 1977). When people think of skin color as a basis for difference and conflict, they usually think of black versus white. However, distinctions made about skin color are more varied than that. Even among African Americans, differences in skin color are noticed and used to make differentiations.
- *Hair styles:* One physical characteristic that is often the source of good or bad impressions or identification with particular groups is a person's hair. Despite a person's other communication, she or he may be accepted or rejected solely because of hair style. There are punk Mohawks, skinheads, and frats. Each is a way of defining differences and acceptance or rejection from specific groups. Such differences are just differences but often become the basis for conflict.
- *Personal hygiene:* People who do not follow social norms concerning body odor, clothing cleanliness, and grooming are often rejected. This becomes the source of some conflicts in schools when other students reject those who do not conform to accepted personal hygiene standards.
- *Dress:* As mentioned, dress can be a way of identifying with particular groups. Gangs have uniforms or colors to define their members. In most schools, there is the in look in clothes. Most often, differences in socioeconomic status are demonstrated by differences in dress. There are fads in fashion—the brand of jeans to wear, the type of clothes to wear to belong to the normal or in-group, and the kind of clothes that the nerds wear. Such differences are normal but often the source of conflict.
- *Specific nonverbal behavior:* Clubs, gangs, and friends often develop specific nonverbal signals that help them signify group identity. Gangs frequently use specific nonverbal signs and signals to identify members. Groups from the Boy and Girl Scouts to sororities and fraternities develop special or secret handshakes and signals. Such signals are used for both identification and seclusion. When used for seclusion, there is potential for conflict.
- *Facial expressions:* Almost everyone has heard the following sentence from their parents: "Don't look at me in that tone of voice!" We all read facial expressions in our attempt to communicate and establish meaning (Ekman, 1992). At times facial expressions are the source of conflict. A look of disgust, anger, or frustration can affect responses from other people, leading to potential conflict. Children learn to insult others by sticking their tongue out

at them, usually invoking a conflict response. We learn to differentiate among a variety of facial expressions and how to respond to them—defensively, aggressively, or supportively.

- *Eye contact:* Along with facial expressions, eye contact is one of the most direct forms of nonverbal communication and varies among cultures (Axtell, 1991). We have expressions such as "If looks could kill . . . " or "His eyes lit up with surprise." We might not trust someone who has shifty eyes. If we can see eye to eye, it implies that we agree. We use eye contact to monitor when people are listening to us or turning us off. When people's eye contact indicates that they are not listening, the basis for conflict exists. We must be careful, however, to remember cultural and gender differences in eye contact. For example, many Native Americans avoid direct eye contact unless they are in a conflict situation. Women tend to avoid direct and continuous eye contact because it is judged as being too direct.
- *Space:* Spatial distance between people has an effect on communication (Hall, 1973, 1981). Various cultures differ in their use of personal, social, and public space when communicating. Personal space in the broader American culture is usually within 18 inches. Social space usually is from 18 to 36 inches, approximately an arm's length away, and public space usually is beyond 36 inches. When people use inappropriate spatial distances for the situation, potential for conflict exists. Probably every parent who has taken a long road trip has had to mediate the conflict that occurs when one child moves across the center line and the other yells, "Mom! He's on my side!" Another aspect of space relates to territoriality. Gangs typically mark out their turf—an area that they consider to be under their domain and control. Very often in schools, various subgroups develop territoriality in playgrounds, lunchrooms, study areas, instructional material centers, seating at sports events, or even seating in classrooms. When students or teachers violate these implicit contracts about what space is to be used by whom, conflict often results. In its most serious form, space or territory conflicts result in physical conflicts and violence (e.g., gang wars). Usually, in schools, space and territory conflicts tend to be verbal. However, they can spill over into disputes off school grounds. Students and teachers must be aware of the importance of space and territory as a potential source of conflict.

SUMMARY

This chapter has introduced sources of conflict and ways that we create and maintain conflict. Also, a number of verbal and nonverbal concepts have been presented. Each is a potential source of creating, maintaining, or exacerbating conflict. Some of the verbal concepts, though used to help manage conflict, may even inflame conflict. These concepts provide the basis for teachers and students to understand potential sources of conflict in their daily lives.

REFERENCES

Adler, A. (1930). Individual psychology. In C. Murchison (Ed.), *Psychologies of 1930*. Worcester, MA: Clark University Press.

Axtell, R. E. (1991). *Gestures*. New York: Wiley.

Ekman, P. (1992). *Telling lies*. New York: Norton.

Gottfredson, L. S. (1981). *Circumscription and compromise: A developmental theory of occupational aspirations. Journal of Counseling Psychology, 18*(6), 545–579.

Hall, E. T. (1981). *Beyond culture*. New York: Doubleday.

Hall, E. T. (1973). *The silent language*. New York: Doubleday.

Hamilton, C., Parker, C., & Smith, D. D. (1982). *Communicating for results.* Belmont, CA: Wadsworth.

Morris, D. (1977). *Manwatching*. New York: Abrams.

Neimeyer, G. J., & Metzler, A. E. (1987). *Sex differences in vocational integration and differentiation. Journal of Vocational Behavior, 30,* 167-174.

CHAPTER 4

Perspectives: Students and Conflict

Students engage in disruptive behaviors that create conflict in classrooms for many reasons. What is needed are ways to assess situations and students so that conflict management can be applied quickly and effectively. The purpose of this chapter is to discuss five key perspectives that provide a basis for teacher assessment of students and to set the stage for effective interactions. The perspectives for assessing students and conflict have physiological, social, psychological, environmental, and observational foundations. All five will be discussed with an eye toward a clearer understanding of why students are involved in conflict and what might be done by teachers to manage conflict.

PHYSIOLOGICAL

The combination of physical growth, psychological development, and environmental change brings with it the potential for student insecurity, fear, anxiety, and conflict. This is most likely in those situations in which students physically or psychologically develop at a different rate than their contemporaries. For example, the seventh-grade boy who is smaller than his peers can become the focal point for jokes. The sixth-grade girl who physically matured faster than her contemporaries may receive unwanted attention and/or teasing. The eighth-grade boy who is particularly large for his age may be expected to respond inappropriately for his age. The psychologically advanced young woman who is very small for her age may be restricted in her activities for the wrong reasons. In each of these cases, unusual physical development influences, and is influenced by, psychological development. Each person's development is determined by the combination and interaction of physical, psychological, and environmental forces. In this section we focus on the part physiology plays in this interaction.

Physiology can be influential in one's ability to function effectively in a school setting, important in conflict development and, when understood by teachers, used to manage conflict. Here we discuss how differential physical growth can lead to conflict; how physiologically based conditions such as diabetes, depression, and hyperactivity can lead to development of conflict; and how alcohol and other drugs can affect one's physiology and lead to conflict.

Size Differences

To be physically *normal* in size, one has to fit into a fairly tight average range. For example, an *average* ninth-grade boy is 5 feet, 6 inches tall. An average ninth-grade girl is 5 feet, 3 inches tall. Consequently, the ninth-grade boy who is 4 feet, 8 inches tall will be viewed as being too small and may be called a "runt" by his peers. The ninth-grade female who is 6 feet tall is likely to viewed as being a "freak." Both descriptions are unfair, possibly damaging, and potentially conflict producing. It is clear that when students grow at a different rate than do their peers, the potential for psychological distance from those peers increases. This psychological distance can lead to feelings of being rejected, unwanted, underloved, or ostracized or can result in alienation or anxiety. When students develop these feelings and/or reactions they are likely to respond in one of four ways. They will withdraw, avoid, attack self, or attack others (Nathanson, 1987). Withdrawal and avoidance can lead to social isolation. When students choose to resolve their personal distress by attacking self or others, then conflict is likely to occur. When this happens, other students become involved, the classroom is likely to be affected, and teachers are forced to respond.

What can be done? Teachers are in a position to educate students about the value of difference and the beauty of diversity. By promoting a positive attitude about differences of all kinds, teachers can set the stage for feeling good about oneself. When this positive attitude is coupled with educational materials that reinforce the value of diversity, students are likely to view their unique differences in a positive light. They will feel good about themselves. Consequently, conflict will be less likely to occur.

Physiological Conditions

Students demonstrate a full range of physical characteristics. Some are normal in all physical attributes. They are physically fit and emotionally secure. By contrast, other students come to school in a physically distressed state. They may have a physical malady that alters their body chemistry in such a way that they cannot concentrate or adequately attend in their environment. Perhaps they just do not feel very good. Participation in school for this latter group can be a challenge. Their physical condition may lead them to become restless, inattentive, overactive, hostile, very emotional, or overly sensitive. If and when they act out their internal states, their behavior can pose a challenge for their classmates and teachers and be the potential source of classroom conflict.

What can be done? The obvious first step is to provide students with physical difficulties every opportunity to receive appropriate medical care. Appropriate medication can help some students achieve normal intellectual and emotional levels. Second, classmates should be educated about the needs of others and ways that these needs might be manifested within a classroom setting. Students who know what others are confronting tend to be very tolerant. Third, teachers can use solution-focused techniques to help distressed students deal with their physical difficulties (see Chapter 8 and deShazer, 1994; O'Hanlon & Weiner-Davis, 1989). Finally, teachers can enlist the services of other school professionals to reduce the conflict-producing impact of physically distressed students. Speech therapists, school psychologists, school counselors, school social workers, and the school nurse, for example, can play instrumental roles in helping distressed students and in reducing potential classroom conflict.

Impact of Alcohol and Other Drugs

The misuse of alcohol and other drugs can lead to physiological distress and interfere with students' abilities to function in a school environment. Alcohol and drug use can change students by altering their cognitive ability to control their emotions, thoughts, and behavior (Gibson & Mitchell, 1986; Muro & Kottman, 1995). It can lead to hostile, aggressive, despondent behavior and to behavior antagonistic to other students and teachers. The obvious result of this type of behavior is conflict in the classroom.

What can be done? Teachers can use a number of different approaches once they have determined a student or group of students have used alcohol and/or other drugs. First, it is helpful to determine the extent of the use. That is, is alcohol or drug use episodic, habitual, excessive, or at a level of addiction? (For an in-depth discussion of these stages, refer to the work of Kinney & Leaton [1978]). An answer to this question can lead to a variety of responses. The determined level of severity will dictate who will be involved and the degree of their involvement. Second, teachers should determine what role they wish to play. That is, would they like to develop a classroom that prevents development of alcohol and drug usage, create a therapeutic setting for students, or focus on an administrative and legal recourse to the problem (Gibson & Mitchell, 1986)? Obviously, teachers might choose to use some combination of these approaches. Third, teachers need to consider who they would like to involve in dealing with the problem. In most schools, a number of resources can be enlisted to confront the problem. Counselors, school psychologists, school social workers, administrators, specialized teachers, specific parents, parent-teacher organizations, and students themselves are some of the resources that might be used. Finally, teachers should not overlook the power that they have to positively influence students. In many situations, teachers serve as the primary adults in students' lives. Students frequently like, respect, and relate to teachers. This relationship between teachers and students can be used to help troubled students directly and, indirectly, to create an educational atmosphere for helping other students positively influence distressed students.

In conclusion, students are influenced by their physiology. Natural growth and development can set the stage for how others respond to them and how they think and feel about themselves. Students' chemical composition can influence who they are and how they act in the school environment. Finally, use of alcohol and other drugs can affect a student's school involvement. All three of these physiological possibilities can lead to conflict in the classroom. Teachers can benefit from awareness of this possibility and from proactively taking steps to prevent or overcome these physiological influences.

SOCIAL

In addition to large reserves of consciously known information, individuals have resources of information at the subconscious or unconscious level (Lee, Pulvino, & Perrone, 1994; Simmons, 1965; Williams, 1964). The total of information known by an individual reflects the individual's formal and informal learning. Two aspects of this learning are particularly important for understanding people: instruction sets and encapsulated units of experience. Both will be discussed in light of conflict and conflict management.

Instruction sets are problem-solving and decision-making strategies that people develop as they attempt to achieve goals. They are analogous to a simple computer program that tells a computer how to add numbers. These instruction sets encompass all aspects of a person's life. For instance, we develop instruction sets for how people should interact, how money should be earned and spent, how people should participate in society, how work should be approached, and how leisure should be enjoyed.

Instruction sets can become patterned responses stimulated by particular events in one's environment. Instruction sets are processes learned informally and without conscious thought, tried, and used repeatedly. **Observation** and **modeling** are key contributors to this learning. For example, the father of one of the authors worked outside the home, his mother inside the home. The author's mother did the grocery shopping for the family, and she would say to her husband, "I need $50 for groceries." Her husband would say, "Here is $25; see what you can do." The author, as a child, frequently observed this interaction. In time, he formed an unconsciously developed instruction set that included the following stereotypical elements: Men control money in the family. Women do the grocery shopping. Having control of money is power. This instruction set remained with the author into his marriage. The author's wife embraced a totally different instruction set, one that said women control the money in the family, both men and women shop for groceries, and the best you can hope for is shared power! The seed for conflict was planted in the author's youth. It did not bloom until 25 years later.

Instruction sets are useful to us. Instruction sets allow us to function effectively without having to create unique reactions for every new situation. This is very helpful in a world in which information proliferation is dramatic and interpersonal interactions are constant. However, responding automatically on instruction sets can be problematic and conflict producing. The previous example demonstrates how this could happen.

Teachers can use knowledge of instruction sets to help manage conflict. By objectifying people's actions, teachers can help them become aware of their unconsciously motivated behavior. Consider the following example in which a teacher hopes to prevent conflict by objectifying and making explicit a student's decision-making style—one instruction set.

TEACHER: I notice that you didn't do well on the most recent quiz.

SAM: I never do when tests are on Mondays.

T: Why do you think you do badly on Monday tests?

SAM: Probably because I don't study on weekends.

T: Is there a particular reason why you don't study on weekends?

SAM: Weekends are for resting and recreating, not for working.

T: I see. How did you arrive at this idea about weekends?

SAM: Well, nobody in my family works on weekends.

T: Have you ever mentioned your belief about weekends to your parents?

SAM: Well, no.

T: What do you think they would say to you if you told them you didn't study for Monday tests because it was a weekend?

SAM: I don't know.

T: Talking with them about this might be helpful to you. Also, if you are concerned about improving how you are doing in class, you might want to rethink your attitude about weekend studying.

SAM: I'll think about it.

The teacher helped explore a belief about weekend studying and offered suggestions that could be helpful to the student. By objectifying the student's behavior, the teacher brought subconsciously motivated behavior to the conscious level. The student might not study for Monday tests in the future, but, because of the teacher's actions, the choice will be a conscious one.

In summary, teachers can help individuals bring instruction sets under their direct conscious control by objectifying and making instruction sets explicit. Teachers also can help others by facilitating their use of positive instruction sets. Students, for example, may have problem-solving or decision-making skills that they use in one aspect of their life but not in others. Teachers could prevent or manage conflict by helping these students adapt functional instruction sets to problematic areas. Teachers can use questions such as the following to help students make this adaptation:

- In other situations, how did you solve the problem?
- If you were at home, how would you solve it?
- If confronted with this as captain of your softball team what would you do?
- Do you know anyone else with a similar problem? How did they try to solve it?
- What skills do you have that would be helpful to you here?

In conclusion, teachers, aware of instruction sets, can be helpful in two ways. They can objectify and make explicit instruction sets that appear to be problematic, and they can facilitate use of positive instruction sets.

In addition to understanding how instruction sets influence people's behavior, it is helpful to understand the role played by encapsulated units of experience. **Encapsulated units of experience** (EUsoE) are occurrences in our lives that have had particular significance. They usually have one or all of the senses connected with them. Whenever a stimulus activates a sensory memory connected with an EUoE, the whole EUoE is activated. A particular smell or sound, for example, can activate a whole memory. Whenever one of the authors drives by a bakery and encounters the smell of warm bread, for example, he has memories of coming home from school and having a snack of his mother's fresh-baked bread with homemade strawberry jam.

We all have positive and negative encapsulated units of experience. These experiences are meaningful and often guide our behavior. A number of encapsulated units of experience can be integrated to form **theme nets**. For example, a child might be congratulated for keeping her room clean, rewarded for being neat, praised for keeping the playroom orderly, and punished for getting her shorts muddy. As result of these individual interactions, or EUsoE, this child might form a theme net for being neat and orderly. It is conceivable that the child's foundational theme net and encapsulated units of experience will be activated by interpersonal interactions later in life.

By understanding the potential impact of encapsulated units of experience and theme nets, teachers can avoid and/or manage conflict. For example, a student may have developed an argumentative theme net. That is, as a child he may have been rewarded, praised, encouraged, commended, or complimented for being argumentative. If the student's behavior in school reflects this theme net, negative school interactions could produce conflict with other students, teachers, or staff. An aware teacher could help the student deconstruct encapsulated units of experience or the theme net by using normal interrogatives of Who? What? When? Where? Why? and How? (Freedman & Combs, 1993; Gorden, 1992). When properly used, these questions will help externalize and make objective the student's experience. The teacher can follow up the student's responses to these questions by focusing on positive ways of reacting (Lee et al., 1994). The following interaction between a teacher and student with a perfectionistic theme net demonstrates the process:

TEACHER: Sarah, as the semester has progressed you have become increasingly nervous. What's happening?

SARAH: It's Jill.

T: What do you mean?

SARAH: Well, as you know, we are working as a team and she isn't serious about what we are doing.

T: Let me see if I understand this. You don't believe that Jill is working as hard on the project as you are or as you would like. Is that it?

SARAH: Yes, that's it.

T: What would you like to have happen?

SARAH: I'd like her to work harder.

T: What would encourage her to work harder?

SARAH: Somebody could tell her to.

T: Who do you want that somebody to be?

SARAH: Well, you, I guess.

T: So, if I told Jill to work harder, you would feel better?

SARAH: I think so.

T: Besides me telling her to work harder, what else could happen?

SARAH: I guess I could talk with her.

T: That's true. You could. Will you?

SARAH: I know I should but I've been putting it off. . . . I will. . . . If it doesn't work, can I talk with you about it?

T: Sure. If your talking doesn't resolve the issue, we'll see what else might be done.

SARAH: Thanks.

In conclusion, instruction sets, encapsulated units of experience, and theme nets can be influential in students' lives. Teachers, aware of these learned responses, can help students examine their needs, wants, and desires by objectifying and making explicit problem-solving and decision-making strategies and by deconstructing encapsulated units of experience and theme nets. By doing so, teachers bring students' motivations to the conscious level and increase the likelihood of positive action. The likelihood of positive action is further increased when teachers successfully encourage others to accept their social responsibility. Ways that this can be accomplished are discussed in the next section.

PSYCHOLOGICAL

There are many ways of explaining why students engage in disruptive behaviors that create conflict in classrooms. What is needed are straightforward, practical ways to assess situations and people so that conflict management can be applied quickly and effectively. Raffini (1980) suggests such a system. Conflict-producing disruptive behavior is a function of needs, emotions, and classroom environmental factors influencing a particular student at a specific moment in time. Any combination of needs, emotions, and environmental pressure can be the occasion for conflict-producing disruptive behavior.

Needs

Maslow (1962) suggests that individuals have a systematic predisposition toward growth that can be viewed as a hierarchy of needs. The most fundamental of these, from the standpoint of survival, are physiological. When these are satisfied, the individual turns toward satisfaction of higher-order needs, including safety and security, love and belongingness, identity and self-esteem. When these needs are satisfactorily achieved, the individual focuses on meeting yet higher-order needs: self-actualization, cognitive needs, and aesthetic needs. Given this wide array of needs, it is easy to speculate that students' conflict-producing disruptive behavior may be to satisfy one or more of their psychological needs. For example, typical needs that students attempt to satisfy are to:

- get attention,
- gain power,
- get even,
- withdraw or avoid, and
- be liked or accepted.

Next you will find examples of a wide array of possible ways that students attempt to satisfy needs and in the process create conflict situations. We acknowledge the limited number of illustrations but trust that the reader will view the following as examples and not as an attempt to be all-encompassing.

Attention Seeking

Whether in the classroom, in the halls, or on school grounds, inevitably more than one student tries to get the attention of others. Skilled attention getters stay within "acceptable" limits in their attempts. Raising one's hand in class, making eye contact, quietly asking a question, and bringing candy for the class are just a few examples of positive attention getters. Negative attention getters range from bringing a weapon to school to talking, even whispering, when one is not supposed to. Various ways of posturing and dressing also draw attention. At the other end of the spectrum are those students who no one remembers. If you took a field trip and they were not on the bus, classmates would not miss them. You possibly would not miss them either until you finished counting and came up one short.

Attention seeking itself is neither bad nor unusual. It is the manner of seeking attention and timing of attention seeking behavior that can cause conflict. However, impulsive children frequently have difficulty following established rules (explicit contracts). You may have to provide gentle but constant and specific reminders.

Gaining Power

Why do some students need to dominate or impose their will on others? Although it is a simplistic explanation, a common characteristic of power seekers is their own insecurity. The class bully is common. Usually bullies do not have anything going for themselves in their role as a student. They do not learn or want to learn. They do not get along with others, maybe because they lack skills but more likely because being top dog is more satisfying than being one of the group. Frequently, bullies need both limits and success in acceptable and valued student behaviors. Helping bullies learn that they can achieve and finding other students who might befriend them is helpful. Because bullies pick on students who are insecure and also physically or emotionally weak, changing a bully's behavior could dramatically improve the life of their victims.

Getting Even

Who does not want to get in the last word? Getting even is motivated by several possible thoughts. "You are not going to get the best of me." "I'm as good as you— maybe better." "If I let you win, I'll never hear the last of it." Getting even, "an eye for an eye," is the antithesis of "turning the other cheek." Getting beaten is a natural outcome of competition, and although only masochists would enjoy getting beaten, a few people who do get beaten want *revenge*. They may want another chance to prove themselves in competition, but getting even means not only beating the other person but making sure that she or he feels the pain. It may contain elements of power (i.e., knowing that *you* inflicted the pain and can do it again). There is a measure of the bully attitude when one wants to get even. This attitude reflects a desire to gain power over another person.

Withdrawing and Avoiding

Students who are never missed or are victims of bullies are two student types who can be classified as withdrawing and avoiding. You can reasonably assume these students are insecure and have been "beaten down." They avoid pain by being invisible and shunning recognition, including teacher praise, because they associate praise with being seen and therefore being vulnerable. You can see why bullies select them as victims and why they suffer quietly—they are well conditioned. Their conditioning often is created by their own actions, experiences, encapsulated units of experience, and theme nets.

Being Liked and Accepted

In a classroom sociogram, there are "stars" and isolates. Stars are in a position to exercise power and control over those who want to be liked—but liked by individuals who are "the" students to be seen with. It is difficult to determine whether certain star qualities cross grades and schools. It is part personality, part physical appearance, yet more than a combination of the two. It is natural to want to be liked, accepted, and loved by those we respect (and of course who are respected by one's peers). When students subject themselves to the misuse of star power, teachers become concerned. When students cling emotionally, and sometimes physically, we cannot help but become concerned. These students are more likely to be neglected than rejected, as is the case with many students who *withdraw* and *avoid* contact.

Emotions

Sometimes a student's conflict-producing behavior is an attempt to deal with emotions. When students have strong feelings, they tend to act them out. This is especially true with younger students. Many emotions may create the underlying motivation for conflict-producing behavior. These four emotions are representative of this wide array:

- Frustration
- Anxiety
- Anger
- Excitement

A number of examples of how conflict arises from students attempting to deal with their emotions follow.

Frustration

Students become frustrated with themselves and with others. The prime source of frustration is disparity between reality and one's expectations. The higher the expectations and greater the distance between performance and expected performance, the greater the frustration. The slippery side of frustration is that it frequently occurs during times of performance or the quest for success. When unsuccessful, people "feel" they are falling behind some internalized schedule. The source of these schedules and their validity for the individual are always questionable. Frustration is different in that we know that the student who is frustrated has imposed an expectation on another person or themselves. Teachers can help students examine their expectations of others and themselves. Also, they can help students understand the relationship among their desires for self, their current level of achievement, and ways to bring the two into congruence. This approach can serve to help students become more realistic about their expectations of self or others.

Anxiety

Anxiety can occur before beginning a task and anywhere along the line toward completing or not completing the task. For any number of reasons, a student "hears" an internal self-dialogue saying, "You can't do it; you never can do it; you're going to fail; everyone is going to know you can't do it." Fear of failure is the primary source of most students' academic anxiety. It also plays a part in athletics and peer relations. Anxiety can be specific to a given task or generalized to everything. **Trait anxiety**, anxiety about everything, would require understanding why the student feels so generally inadequate. **State anxiety**, anxiety centered on the given task, requires focusing on the task and how it is perceived by the student. When anxiety completely takes over and the person is psychologically and physically paralyzed, fear sets in. Before addressing the anxiety, the fear has to be addressed. Psychological support and concern, even guaranteed protection from the source of one's fear, may be needed.

Anger

An anger response is a learned response to a noxious situation. More specifically, anger is composed of physiological reactions, feelings, thoughts, memories, and motor responses linked with escape from an unpleasant or stressful situation. McKay, Rogers, and McKay (1989) believe that the sole function of anger is to stop stress. They suggest four kinds of stress that anger serves to dissipate: painful affect, painful sensation, frustrated drive, and threat (p. 46). Each of these categorical responses can be stimulated in many ways. For example, an angered response to painful affect can serve to ward off anxiety, fear, loss, depression, hurt, shame, or feelings of failure, badness, or unworthiness. In a like manner, an angry response to painful sensation can occur when one is rushed or pushed too hard, physically injured, overstimulated, tired or overworked, or physically tense. In school situations, frustrated drives can result in displayed anger when students have needs or drives thwarted, when things do not go as students would like, or when students feel forced to do or be in ways different than they desire. Student anger also can occur when students feel attacked, engulfed, or abandoned.

What can teachers do to help students overcome the negative consequences of anger and to help them learn more effective coping mechanisms? McKay et al. (1989) and Potter-Efron (1994) offer a number of ways teachers can assist students. For example, teachers can help students develop more effective ways of interacting with others, teach them strategies for taking care of their needs by themselves, help them develop new sources of psychological support, teach students to negotiate assertively and effectively, and, if these approaches do not work, teach students how to let go.

Beyond direct work with students, teachers can further develop their skills in helping students deal with anger by becoming familiar with specific programs designed to teach students strategies and techniques for dealing with anger. One such approach is an anger-coping program offered by Lochman, Dunn, and Klimes-Dougan (1993). This program uses cognitive-behavioral principles to teach students to cope with anger. A second program, **aggression replacement training**, uses behavioral, affective, and cognitive strategies to help students respond to feelings of others, identify anger-provoking triggers, communicate with others in a positive way, and learn to handle conflict without fighting (Goldstein & Glick, 1987). Familiarity with materials in these programs, and similar ones, can help teachers assist students in coping with anger-eliciting stimuli and overcoming anger responses.

Excitement

Students become excited when anticipating a positive experience without knowing exactly how and when they will have the experience. The positive experience is not guaranteed, but there is much better than an even chance that it will happen, and in the student's mind, it will be an enjoyable experience. In addition to being positive, the anticipated experience may be a first-time experience, a slightly different previous experience, or the repeat of a completely enjoyable prior experience. As students and the anticipated experience approach, the level of excitement rises to where it may take over the student's entire being.

Several experiences can enlist this type of reaction. A birthday party, taking the driver's license test, the big game, and high school graduation, for example, can engender excitement for those anticipating success and joy but frustration and anxiety for those who anticipate failure.

ENVIRONMENTAL

School and classroom environments have an effect on students' behaviors. To understand how environments affect students' needs and emotions, it is necessary to make a concentrated effort to see the environment from a student's perspective. Most schools and classrooms are designed and decorated from an adult perspective, that is, from what teachers and administrators think will please students. Student and adult perspectives may not be the same. As discussed in Chapter 2, each role we play has an affect on the implicit and explicit contracts that are operative at any point in time. Although teachers, administrators, and parents often think that when students are at school they will be in the role of student, that may only be true during specific environments and circumstances for the child. During school time, they also occupy the roles of friend, playmate during recess or free time, colleague when working in study groups, or athlete during gym class. As the examples indicate, each environmental change has an effect on the role played and the implicit and explicit contracts in effect. It is unrealistic to expect students to feel and act the same throughout the school day when the environment and accompanying roles change.

The several environments in school take quite different forms (structure) and serve unique functions. Students are expected to understand or learn what behaviors are acceptable and unacceptable as they move across environments. Taking classrooms as an example, rules guiding behavior tend to be teacher specific as well as subject specific. It actually may prove more difficult for some students to adapt to differences between classrooms than to the differences in acceptable behaviors when moving from a classroom, through the hall, into the bathroom, to the lunchroom, and then to the gym or playground. For some, it is nearly impossible to adapt behavior appropriate to varying physical settings, changes in who constitutes the peer group, and the teacher who is in charge.

Different school environments impose certain rules (explicit contracts) of behavior relative to the task at hand to ensure that students and staff are physically safe and psychologically secure and that a sense of community or belonging exists for everyone. Physical safety (being safe) takes precedence over all else, and psychological safety (feeling safe) takes precedence over community adult standards. Conflicts seem inevitable given these differences.

Both environments and teachers differ in the amount of self-control or self-discipline students are expected to exercise to function effectively. The variance among teachers and among settings imposes different degrees of psychological structure through the number and type of rules (implicit and explicit contracts) and physically through real and imagined barriers that are established.

Witkin and Goodenough (1981) were among the earliest researchers to identify two basic types of learners: those who need more psychological and physical structure from teachers to learn and those who need less teacher-imposed structure. They found that those needing more structure were more easily distracted when working on a task and that these distractions could be visual, verbal, or physical. Possibly the best example of how physical structure affects learning was evident during the era when schools went from closed, individual classrooms to open learning modules. Many students who were able to concentrate and stay on task in individual classrooms floundered. However, students who were capable of managing diverse stimuli actually thrived.

The reason for briefly focusing on how different environments affect students' attitudes and behaviors is to underscore the thought that not all conflicts are interpersonal. There are personal-environmental conflicts that need attention. To this point we have discussed needs, emotions, and environmental factors as potential sources for disruptive behavior. We will now turn our attention to ways to determine how personalities contribute to conflict. Also, we will suggest a way that teachers can prepare themselves for dealing with conflict.

OBSERVATIONAL

Nonverbal behaviors and postures can be used both to understand people's basic personality structures as well as to help assess potential conflict situations. Tomkins

(1979), for instance, offers observations about ways in which people evidence positive, neutral, or negative characteristics as a reflection of their emotional state. He suggests that interest and/or excitement is expressed by the person's eyebrows being down, the obvious tracking of the eyes, and the intense listening posture. When a person is surprised or startled, raised eyebrows and blinking eyes are evident. Fear is accompanied by a frozen stare, a pale face, profuse sweating, and erect hair. Anger can be seen in a person's frown, clenched jaw, and red face. Shame is shown by the eyes being down, the head down and averted, and the blush on the face. People provide information about what they are emotionally experiencing through their nonverbal mannerisms. They tell the world how they feel about themselves and how they wish to be taken through their postures and gestures (Morris, 1977; Walton, 1989). This point is true for people who feel good about themselves and those who do not.

As members of society, we have learned to identify basic differences in the ways people present themselves. Most would agree that people with poor self-concepts and low self-esteem act in a withdrawn manner. They may have poor postures. Their general posture is usually out of balance. They may stand or sit hunched over in a self-protective mode. Often, their heads are thrust forward and down rather than aligned with their spinal columns. Such people frequently are uncomfortable with their hands and arms. When standing, they often stick their hands in their pockets or fold them in front of themselves. Their nonverbal behavior often invites others to pick on them. On the other hand, belligerent, angry people have different postures. Such people stand leaning forward slightly and with their jaws jutted forward. It is almost as if they are taking a stance daring someone to hit them. Their gait is stiff, and nonverbal language is pointed and sharp.

Axtell (1991) suggests that individuals communicate with all elements of their bodies. They share their inner beliefs through their head and face, eyes, ears, nose, cheeks, lips and mouth, chin, arms, hands, fingers, legs and feet, and their whole body (p. 59). Ekman (1992) goes as far as to say that individuals communicate so powerfully through nonverbal clues that it is possible to tell whether an individual is being honest or deceitful. He suggests that the messages are there if we know how to read them. Dobson (1980) provides a relatively straightforward way of examining posture that can be used for understanding people and for assessing potential conflicts.

Terry Dobson spent his life studying aikido and its possible applications to everyday life. He helped others live more constructive lives and manage conflict by applying principles from the Japanese culture that are integral to aikido. Symbolism regarding squares, circles, and triangles was used in this way. Figure 4–1 shows a brief summary of Dobson's reflections of how squares, circles, and triangles can be applied to understanding people. Please note that each geometric figure has certain personality characteristics associated with it.

People can have too much or too little of the figures in their personalities or need more of a figure in their personalities. Each of the figures and their personality relationships are examined relative to body language, verbal expression, and general attitude/spirit. Six problem types are outlined in Figure 4–2.

Being balanced is having an equal amount of each of the shapes and/or having the ability to use the appropriate amount of each shape when needed. Being balanced is

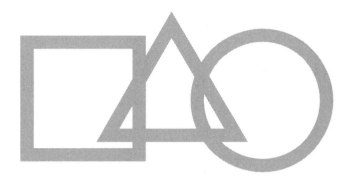

Square: The square is characterized by balance. It is a shape that depicts solidity and strength. As a verb, square means to mend, as in "square things up"; to reconcile, as in "make things square again"; or to resolve and settle, as in "to square things between us."

Triangle: The triangle, because of its sharp points at the corners, depicts focus with a strong base. The visual energy of the triangle seems to concentrate, aim, or converge toward one or more of its points.

Circle: A circle depicts adaptability and wholeness. Circles encompass, surround, and envelop areas. They also can be wheels or balls that can turn, adapt, and flow with any terrain.

Figure 4–1
Personality characteristics symbolized by the square, triangle, and circle

indicative of being centered. The term **centered** refers to the process of integrating the various aspects of yourself—your body, mind, and spirit—into a unified whole. Practically, this results in your complete awareness of the moment, your total presence in it. When you are centered, you can do the right thing at the right moment. Later, you may be slightly surprised at how effortlessly you handled the situation. The process of centering may be a slow, deliberate procedure, or it may be accomplished in an instant. Regardless, when you are centered you are balanced (square), focused (triangle), and adaptable (circle). As said in aikido, "Everything balances around the center and centers around balance." Having the ability to center oneself is key in responding to and managing conflict situations. Centering is part of a variety of strategies to manage conflict.

Centered body language: Balanced, natural, relaxed, body posture aligned with gravity; gestures appropriate to the situation

Centered verbal expression: Short, simple, to-the-point statements; even tone of voice; blending or active listening responses, with a focus on others

Centered attitude/spirit: Inquisitive, spontaneous, adaptable, alert

In conclusion, nonverbal behavior provides clues about individuals in general and students in particular. By attending to nonverbal information, teachers can gain

Figure 4–2
Personality problem types

Too Much Square

Body language: Rigid, tight, symmetrical, braced

Verbal expression: "No way!" "Not me!" "That's not the way we do it around here!"

Attitude/spirit: Sullen, defensive, negative

Too Much Triangle

Body language: Chin thrust forward, pointing and jabbing, sharp

Verbal expression: "Do it my way!" "That's an order!" "You better do it right next time!"

Attitude/spirit: Angry, arrogant, competitive

Too Much Circle

Body language: Shifts, squirms, and fidgets, much head and eye movement

Verbal expression: "I'll think about it." "I'll call you next week."

Attitude/spirit: Vague, elusive, hard to pin down

Not Enough Square

Body language: Many gestures, much nervous energy, restless

Verbal expression: "You're asking too much!" "That's not my responsibility!" "Can't you see I'm busy?"

Attitude/spirit: Edgy, erratic, skittish

Not Enough Triangle

Body language: Much grooming, much movement, hesitant gestures, starts but may not finish

Verbal expression: "Well, I'm not sure...what do you think?" "But on the other hand..." "I guess it was my fault."

Attitude/spirit: Hesitant, flighty, hot and cold

Not Enough Circle

Body language: Serious, intense demeanor; little smiling or small talk; asymmetrical posture

Verbal expression: "Do you want this job or not?" "When you're ready to cooperate, I'll be here!" "I don't care what Mr. Smith said."

Attitude/spirit: Relentless, unyielding, single-minded

a better understanding of students' needs and a clearer idea about the meaning of their behavior. They can use this knowledge to manage conflict by helping students meet their needs in socially appropriate ways.

SUMMARY

In this chapter, we discussed five significant contributions to individuals and conflict that focus on physiological, social, psychological, environmental, and observational perspectives. In discussing the physiological perspective, emphasis was placed on size differences, physiological conditions such as hyperactivity, and the impact of alcohol and other drugs. Emphasis in the social domain was centered on instruction sets, encapsulated units of experience, and theme nets. Focus of the psychological domain was on how student needs and emotions influence behavior and effect generation of conflict. In discussing environmental considerations, school environments were discussed from the perspective of rules and contracts. Observational considerations centered on the importance of attending to nonverbal information. These variables were examined to offer a partial explanation of why students behave as they do. Finally, we presented a way of assessing people and the way personalities contribute to creating conflict.

REFERENCES

Axtell, R. E. (1991). *Gestures*. New York: Wiley.

deShazer, S. (1994). *Words were originally magic*. New York: Norton.

Dobson, T. (1980) *When push comes to shove: handling problem people*. Unpublished workshop materials.

Ekman, P. (1992). *Telling lies*. New York: Norton.

Freedman, J., & Combs, G. (1993). Invitations to new stories: Using questions to explore alternate possibilities. In S. G. Gilligan & R. Price (Eds.), *Therapeutic conversations* (pp. 291–303). New York: Norton.

Gibson, R. L., & Mitchell, M. H. (1986). *Introduction to counseling and guidance* (2nd ed.). Upper Saddle River, NJ: Prentice Hall.

Goldstein, A. P., & Glick, B. (1987). *Aggression replacement training: A comprehensive intervention for aggressive youth*. Champaign, IL: Research Press.

Gorden, R. (1992). *Basic interviewing skills*. Itasca, IL: Peacock.

Kinney, J., & Leaton, G. (1978). *Loosening the grip: A handbook of alcohol information*. St. Louis: Mosby.

Lee, J. L., Pulvino, C. J., & Perrone, P. A. (1994). *Dynamic counseling*. Minneapolis: Educational Media Corporation.

Lochman, J. E., Dunn, S. E., & Klimes-Dougan, B. (1993). *An intervention and consultation model from a social cognitive perspective: A description of the anger coping program. School Psychology Review, 22*(3), 458-471.

Maslow, A, (1962). *Toward a psychology of being.* New York: Van Nostrand.

McKay, M., Rogers, P., & McKay, J. (1989). *When anger hurts.* New York: MJF.

Morris, D. (1977). *Manwatching.* New York: Abrams.

Muro, J. J., & Kottman, T. (1995). *Guidance and counseling in the elementary and middle schools.* Dubuque, IA: Brown.

Nathanson, D. (1987). The shame/pride axis. In H. B. Lewis (Ed.), *The role of shame in symptom formation* (pp. 183–205). Hillsdale, NJ: Erlbaum.

O'Hanlon, W. H., & Weiner-Davis, M. (1989). *In search of solutions.* New York: Norton.

Potter-Efron, R. (1994). *Angry all the time.* New York: MJF.

Raffini, J. (1979). *Managing surface behavior of children in schools.* Unpublished workshop materials, University of Wisconsin–Whitewater.

Simmons, C. M. (1965). *Your subconscious power.* North Hollywood, CA: Wilshire.

Tomkins, S. S. (1979). Script theory; differential magnification of affects. In H. E. Howe & R. A. Dienstbier (Eds.), *Nebraska symposium of motivation* (Vol. 26, pp. 201–236). Lincoln: University of Nebraska Press.

Walton, D. (1989). *Are you communicating?* New York: McGraw-Hill.

Williams, J. K. (1964). *The wisdom of your subconscious mind.* Upper Saddle River, NJ: Prentice Hall.

Witkin, H. A., & Goodenough, D. R. (1981). *Cognitive styles: Essence and origins.* New York: International Universities Press.

CHAPTER 5

Managing Conflict

Conflicts occur at many levels in schools. They occur among students, teachers, parents, administrators, and staff. Managing conflict is the focus of this chapter. We concentrate on conflict management strategies that can be used by teachers.

Conflict can be handled in many ways. Some of the methods presented in the literature are short-term solutions, others long-term. Although we will mention some of the short-term solutions, we will concentrate on long-term perspectives. We do this because we believe that short-term solutions usually are less useful in settings in which people are expected to interact over an extended period of time. Schools are one of these settings. Students and teachers typically work together intensively for a 9- or 10-month period and may be together for a number of years. Because we take a long-term perspective, we believe that in a two-party conflict situation, both parties ultimately must view the interaction positively. For this to happen, the teacher must provide a basis for harmony that is built on a foundation of trust and respect. Three cornerstones of this foundation are provided by Bolton (1979, 222–223). He suggests that people can help others resolve conflicts if they:

1. treat the other person with respect,
2. listen until they experience the other side and are able to reflect content, feelings, and meanings accurately, and
3. are able to state briefly their own views, needs, and feelings.

We believe that teachers can assume Bolton's general guidelines. By employing these attitudes, teachers will communicate their care and respect for students. This positive attitude sets the stage for a facilitative working relationship. We are not suggesting that this positive attitude *automatically* leads to positive outcomes but rather that if a person takes a negative perspective, he or she *almost* always will experience a negative outcome. When a negative perspective is adopted, a positive outcome is an exception.

Bolton offers a process for managing conflict. First, one must listen to the other person with respect and speak in noninflammatory tones. This helps both parties focus on important central issues and defuses uncontrollable, negative emotions. Second, one should offer a specific way of discussing the issue in question and ask the other person whether they would be willing to try this way of relating. This approach initially focuses on the method to be used in relating rather than on the more emotionally ladened issue. It also provides an opportunity for joint commitment to resolution and enlists the other person in resolving the conflict. Finally, one can attempt to establish when an issue will be discussed. This provides an opportunity for discussing issues when things are less intense and emotional. By adhering to these steps, an individual can help another focus on important issues in a way that reduces threat, diffuses the potentially negative impact of emotions, and provides a means for mutually managing conflict.

Weeks (1992) reinforces Bolton's perspective in his "conflict-partnership pathway to effective conflict resolution" (p. 70). His approach clearly emphasizes cooperation, shared responsibility, respect, and desire for both (all) parties to have their needs met through positive interactions. Weeks suggests that conflict management consists of systematically creating an atmosphere conducive to shared problem solving and conflict resolution by adhering to the following eight basic steps:

1. Create an effective atmosphere.
2. Clarify perceptions.
3. Focus on individual and shared needs.
4. Build shared positive power.
5. Look to the future, then learn from the past.
6. Generate options.
7. Develop "doable" stepping stones to action.
8. Make mutual-benefit agreements.

CONFLICT MANAGEMENT STRATEGIES

Conflict frequently is approached in several ways. Bolton (1979) states that individuals are likely to approach conflict situations from one of four perspectives. He suggests that they will deny the existence of conflict, recognize it but avoid getting involved in resolving it, give in or capitulate to others, or try to dominate others to get their desires and goals met. Weeks (1992) adds to these possibilities. He believes that in some conflict situations individuals will attempt to bargain to get their needs met or use short-term, stopgap measures to reduce conflict. He terms this latter strategy a "Band-Aid approach."

We have identified 10 specific strategies that broaden Bolton's offerings and expand on Weeks's "pathway to conflict resolution," ones that are typically employed for reducing conflict. In presenting them, we first review the four that are most **passive**. These are followed by three relatively **assertive** approaches. The final three we believe to be the most **facilitative.** Of these three, we favor the confluent response. We present it last only because we elaborate on it more fully in the next chapter. In presentation of all strategies, we briefly describe when to use the strategy, provide rules for using it, explain how to use it, and then present an example in which the strategy is applied.

It should be noted that the 10 strategies all have utilitarian value. Some have wide generalizability. Others are much more limited in application. We believe that the confluent response is useful in most situations. By contrast, we view the forcing approach to have a more limited application. When using the forcing approach, one must be extremely careful to maintain ethical procedures. Having noted these two exceptions, we present all 10 strategies without placing higher value on some more than others.

In illustrating the 10 strategies with specific examples, we have selected examples that represent a wide array of teacher interactions. Although most examples revolve around teacher-student interactions, some reflect conflict management between teachers and parents, administrators, and staff. In most examples, teachers are viewed as being facilitators of harmony. However, in a few the intent is to show how teachers can use a specific strategy to manage conflict in which they are personally involved. In presenting examples, we indicate how one conflict resolution strategy could be applied. We do not believe that all strategies fit all situations or that there is only one strategy for each situation. In most situations, several strategies could be used effectively to restore harmony.

PASSIVE STRATEGIES

Doing Nothing

When to Do Nothing

Doing nothing is a neutral conflict management option (Dobson & Miller, 1974). Sometimes taking a wait-and-see attitude is best. This option allows you time to size up the situation, observe the issues without being embroiled in them, and provides time to determine an appropriate course of action. Also, in some situations, the passage of time allows conflict to diminish of its own accord. The worst thing to do in trying to be helpful is breathe life back into an argument that is losing steam. As a rule of thumb, a good time to work on compromises is when combatants are exhausted. By doing nothing, you might allow participants to reach a point when they will be open to your involvement, a point when they welcome compromise. Usually, if no one is in danger of being hurt physically or psychologically, you can wait. Finally, if one of the combatants believes you favor the other side, you may want to delay becoming directly involved until this issue can be resolved. If it cannot, a neutral party may be called for.

Rules for Doing Nothing

On the surface, doing nothing is simple. Your primary objective is to remain uninvolved in the conflict. However, your emotions might interfere with your dispassionate observation. The primary ways your emotions can be regulated are to focus on:

- remaining centered,
- maintaining a calm and quiet demeanor, and
- listening attentively.

How to Do Nothing

Contrary to the name of this option, doing nothing requires that you take active control of your emotions and behavior. This can be done if you are clear as to why you are choosing this option and understand the positive benefits that can accrue if you are successful, namely, avoiding or forestalling destructive confrontation. The option of doing nothing is based on a positive view of yourself and your right to make appropriate choices in your life. It must be remembered that doing nothing is a choice, a choice that you make because you determine that it is the best course of action to take. Doing nothing is a choice made from strength, not weakness.

Specifically, when choosing this option:

- center and focus yourself,
- be aware of your emotions,
- control your verbal and nonverbal behavior,
- attend to verbal and nonverbal behavior, and
- thoughtfully prepare how you would like to communicate to restore harmony.

EXAMPLE

Conflict: Between teacher and student

The problem: A student in a classroom setting who continuously "stretches the limits" to get attention establishes conditions for conflict between teacher and student. The student takes longer than needed to sit in his seat, ambles up to the pencil sharpener, and fails to get class material ready in a timely manner. When the teacher addressed this behavior in the past, the student seemed to enjoy the attention. Consequently, the teacher decides to try doing nothing.

The doing nothing approach: In this approach, the teacher purposely resists acknowledging or attending to the student's behavior. By focusing on the rest of the class and class activities and doing nothing about the student's annoying but unharmful behavior, the teacher can diminish what the student is seeking: attention for acting out. If this conflict resolution approach fails to diminish the student's negative behavior, an assertive intervention could be used (i.e., confrontation, standing firm, or forcing).

Withdrawing

When to Use Withdrawing

If reason and maneuvering are not going to work, look for a way out (Dobson & Miller, 1974; Hamilton, Parker, & Smith, 1982; Johnson & Johnson, 1991). In a life-threatening situation, get the attention of others by whatever means it takes. If you are being unduly criticized, leave with as much grace and pride as you can muster. For example, "Excuse me, this is uncomfortable and unproductive; I am leaving." Exit quickly without looking back.

Similarly, it is helpful to provide students with an exit that allows them to feel safe and save face, while allowing you to be in control of the conflict situation. If you find yourself being the aggressor, you can change the atmosphere to reduce tension.

Rules for Withdrawing

First, remove yourself from the conflict situation as quickly as possible. Do not hesitate. Second, leave purposefully. That is, do not be ambiguous in your actions or words. Leave the interaction with clear intention and purpose.

How to Withdraw

Is this the time to withdraw? If you cannot reason or maneuver, the conflict is heating up, and there is a way out, take it. You may have to decide to act quickly. Be prepared to do so. Stay centered. Avoid letting your ego turn the conflict into an impossible confrontation. Withdraw with clear intention and purpose. This is not a sign of weakness but an indication that you are both willing and able to make a specific choice. Walk away. Remember, you are exercising your right to stay out of destructive situations.

EXAMPLE

Conflict: Between teacher and parent

The problem: A teacher is asked to hold a conference with a parent concerning ways to increase the student's academic success. The teacher willingly attends this meeting. In the meeting the parent refuses to discuss what can be done by involved parties to assure student success. Rather, the parent focuses on personally attacking the teacher. All efforts by the teacher to focus on academic methods are refuted and followed by further attacks on the teacher.

The withdrawing approach: Since the teacher in this example is in a no-win situation, an appropriate strategy is to remove him- or herself from verbal abuse. The teacher could rightfully employ the conflict resolution strategy of withdrawal. By attending the scheduled meeting, the teacher conveys a willingness to work on the student's problem. By using withdrawal, the teacher communicates that he or she will work professionally in the student's behalf but will not be attacked personally.

Smoothing

When to Use Smoothing

Although specific goals may be important, in the smoothing approach, the most important outcome is maintenance or enhancement of the existing interpersonal relationship (Hamilton et al., 1982; Johnson & Johnson, 1991). The belief foundational to this approach is that conflict cannot be resolved by individuals who are antagonistic to each other. Rather, it is believed that meaningful conflict management only will occur when involved individuals have their needs met, respect individuals with whom they are involved, and value the interpersonal relationship. Because smoothing is aimed at keeping people happy, it might be the conflict management option of choice in situations in which short- or long-term threats to interpersonal relationships exist.

Rules for Using Smoothing

The main goal is to keep people happy and involved in the conflict management process. To do this, one must (a) avoid antagonistic words, (b) create an atmosphere in which all ideas are entertained openly, (c) avoid saying anything that can be taken negatively, (d) be prepared to set personal goals or objectives aside, and (e) do whatever is necessary to maintain the relationship.

How to Use Smoothing

The smoothing approach is most effective when it uses counseling principles of awareness, observation, blending, and pacing (Lee, Pulvino, & Perrone, 1994). In this approach, the teacher focuses attention on students or others in the conflict situation, to determine their needs, wants, goals, or desires. When these elements are determined, they are used by the teacher as the basis for blending with individuals and for leading them to manage conflict. Consider the following as an example of this approach: A student wants to miss an exam to go on a field trip, whereas the teacher would prefer that the student take the exam with the class and forego the field trip.

TEACHER: What would you like to have happen?

SCOT: I'd like to be able to go on the field trip.

T: I can tell that the field trip is important to you.

SCOT: Yes, it is.

T: I can understand that. I'm curious though, what do you think about missing the test?

SCOT: Well, there will be more tests; there may not be any more field trips.

T: Can I interpret that to mean that you don't think it is important that you take this test?

SCOT: Well, it isn't that important, is it?

T: I think it is. However, I don't think that you going on the field trip necessarily means that you can't take the test.

SCOT: What do you mean?

T: I think we can figure out a way where you can do both.

SCOT: That would be great.

T: OK, here is what we will do. . . .

EXAMPLE

Conflict: Between teacher and student

The problem: A student who has had difficulty in committing himself to the work necessary to succeed turns in an assignment on Friday that was due on Wednesday. The teacher had previously set a policy for all work being turned in on time.

The Smoothing Approach: The teacher would like to break the student's negative attitude toward school and schoolwork. Although the teacher is disappointed that the assignment is late, she is happy that the student has turned it in at all. Consequently, the teacher accepts the assignment without penalizing the student for tardiness. By accepting the assignment in this manner, she demonstrates the underlying principle of the smoothing approach: maintenance of the relationship is more important than other outcomes. Hopefully, the teacher's actions will lead to future positive actions by the student.

Diversion

When to Use Diversion

Diversion changes the flow of energy. In a physical conflict situation, it could be a counterattack or feint that draws the attacker's attention away from his or her primary objective: completion of the attack. Diversions can be surprising, distracting, or amusing. They are used to reduce the intensity and emotional tone of the attack so that movement can be made toward restoring harmony (Dobson & Miller, 1974).

Diversion is a means for helping students reduce intensity, disengage, or refocus their energy. If the issue is not serious or life-threatening, and if students respect you and your position, then any form of diversion probably will work. The simplest way to use diversion is to surprise students by behaving in an unexpected manner. For instance, if they expect you to be upset, you can surprise them by being calm and reasoning. By distracting students, you get them to shift their attention. This provides you an opportunity to take control of the interaction. The surprising thing in this strategy is that you do not have to get students to focus on something terribly meaningful, just get them to shift their attention. This is exemplified by parents who spend time with infant children distracting and surprising them with games like "peek-a-boo." Humor is one of the great distracters. Finding ways to put an amusing twist on a situation can reduce tension, help people laugh at themselves and/or the situation, and provide a means for you to help resolve differences harmoniously.

Rules for Using Diversion

Diversion depends on your ability to assess a situation, determine an appropriate response, and deliver your message in a timely manner. For some people, their ability to see humor will be their greatest ally in using diversion. For others, the ability to think quickly of alternatives to meet needs in the situation will be the ammunition needed for diversion. For still others, knowing when to use diversion might be their greatest strength. There is not a right or best way to employ diversion. Each person has to use their unique skills, assessment of the situation, and timing to use diversion as a conflict management strategy.

Although diversion can be used in unique ways, a few general rules for using it are as follows:

- Center yourself. Slow yourself mentally and physically.
- Assess the situation, including all involved individuals.
- Consider courses of actions and their potential consequences.
- Consider timing of your response.
- Respond assertively.

How to Divert

Diversion is easiest and usually most effective when you use a simple strategy that is either believable or solicits an automatic response. For instance, you can use diversion nonverbally by moving, pointing, or focusing attention on something/someone else. This can be accomplished by making an interesting observation or comment about the object of your focus.

- "Boy, if first-graders saw you sixth-graders acting like this, what would they think?"
- "Whoa, what's going on here? Yesterday you two were best friends."
- "Let's save this for gym class."

You can divert by making a humorous comment about the situation. Remember, however, that care must be used with humor so that it is not seen as a put-down.

- "Let me guess—you two are putting on a show for the class about a fight scene from a TV program last night. I'm confused—which one of you is supposed to be the good guy? How did it turn out?"
- "Is that the maddest face you can make? Come on, even I can do better than that!"

If the situation seems appropriate (i.e., the situation is not serious), you can create a diversion by asking one or more of the persons involved in the conflict situation to continue and amplify their conflict behavior. Under some circumstances, this form of diversion can diffuse a conflict situation. For example, you might have students "act out" their disagreement but in slow motion so you can control their behavior by moderating the tempo. When they have to focus on slowing down, their protracted thinking will serve to lessen the emotional tension, give pause for thought, and, more important, may provide them an opportunity to see how they look to others.

Carried to an extreme, you can create a miniature psycho-drama. You could have conflicting students select another student to perform in their behalf in simulated verbal interchange with another performer. Both actors can be directed by the original students. The actors can be instructed by the conflicting students to explain why they should act in specific ways. You can serve as the director to assure that the scenario is played out in a way that is consistent with the original conflict. This approach can have great power because it provides the conflicting students an opportunity to distance themselves from their emotions in the situation while allowing them a chance to gain an alternate perception of events.

Still another approach is to videotape a conflict and have conflicting students critique it while it is played back. As teacher-director, you can ask for explanations and raise questions to direct their learning.

EXAMPLE

Conflict: Between two students, with teacher as facilitator

The problem: Two students who are working on a project become agitated with each other. The teacher believes that the students can benefit from their interaction, that they are very creative in accomplishing their project, and consequently she would like to keep them together on their project.

The diversion approach: The teacher wants to divert the students from focusing on negative aspects of their relationship. To do this, she announces to the class that the twosome has taken a creative approach to working on their project, one that could benefit other teams. By using diversion to focus on the positive, the teacher can help hold negative outbreaks to a minimum.

ASSERTIVE STRATEGIES

Confronting

When to Confront

The confronting approach to conflict management is useful when tension exists between individuals. This approach is especially important when tension is impeding progress toward goal achievement for all involved parties (Johnson & Johnson, 1991). It focuses on problem solving by deliberately facing issues that are preventing solution. Confronting is an open, out-front approach that treats all participants equally and depends on open, honest communication and mutual respect and trust between (among) participants. When these ingredients are present, confrontation is appropriate.

Rules for Confronting

The operational rules for confronting are to be (a) open, (b) honest, (c) fair, and (d) straightforward in verbal interchanges. Focus on clarifying the feelings of all participants and helping them discuss what they would like to accomplish. Work toward finding solutions that will satisfy emotional and cognitive needs of all participants.

How to Confront

The confronting approach is a "put the cards on the table" approach. It assumes that individuals have enough self-esteem and ego strength to deal with conflict in a growthful, productive way. Given this belief, confrontation should be direct, purposeful, honest, and flexible. It should be approached with thoughtful care and caring. All parties should be given an opportunity to contribute to the process. All ideas and inputs should be valued.

EXAMPLE

Conflict: Between teacher and student

The problem: A student is disruptive in class by talking out of turn in class discussions, talking repeatedly, and making disparaging remarks about others.

The confronting approach: The teacher asks the student to remain after class. At this point, the teacher confronts the student with the observed behaviors and shares his negative reaction to those behaviors. The teacher facilitates an open discussion while focusing the student on her actions and what can be done to develop more positive behaviors.

Forcing

When to Force

Forcing is a conflict management approach that attempts to end conflict by controlling what will be done. It is a contest of power. Individuals using this approach probably hold the belief that one has to lose for another to succeed. Consequently, to avoid losing, they exert power to achieve their goals. Individuals emphasize personal goal achievement and expend little or no effort in attempting to preserve the relationship. The forcing approach is the opposite of smoothing in terms of goals and process. It is totally goal oriented and unconcerned with relationships. This approach should be used when conflict is viewed as being a win-lose situation, when an individual is content with others losing as long as he or she wins, and when maintenance of the relationship is not important (Hamilton et al., 1982; Johnson & Johnson, 1991).

Rules for Forcing

The forcing approach employs power to achieve outcomes. In using this approach, an individual seeks his or her goals, even at potentially high interpersonal cost. To do this, assertive or even aggressive tactics can be employed. Attacking others' weaknesses, overpowering them, or intimidation are all acceptable methods. The most significant rule of this approach is for an individual to force his or her preferred solution through any legal or ethical means available.

How to Force

The purpose of using the forcing approach is to win any way possible. Winning is more likely to occur when opponents are viewed as being ineffective in building or communicating their case. The main method for accomplishing this subgoal is by controlling pertinent information and by using ingredients of persuasion such as authority, reciprocation, scarcity, commitment, consistency, and social proof (Cialdini, 1988).

EXAMPLE

Conflict: Between teacher and student

The problem: Teachers are required to enforce the following school rule: "No hats or coats can be worn in school. No Walkmen can be used in school. There are no exceptions to this rule."

The forcing approach: The teacher is obligated by contract to enforce this rule. A student who breaks the rule knows the consequences. By enforcing the rule, the teacher forces any student to obey the rule or pay the consequences.

Standing Firm

When to Stand Firm

When there is no other option, standing firm is appropriate (Dobson & Miller, 1974). In doing so, you should be prepared for the worst possible consequences while working toward achieving harmony as soon as possible. Even in dire circumstances, conflict can be managed (Markova, 1991).

When threatened physically, our natural survival instinct of **fight or flight** is triggered. When someone belittles us, verbally puts us down, or unduly criticizes us, we first tend to become psychologically threatened, then may respond by standing up for our rights. In this type of situation, you have other options, probably ones that would be preferable. However, when physically threatened, it may be necessary to stand firm when you have no path for flight. If this is the case, then do so in a way that will bring the conflict to resolution as soon and amicably as possible. Do not escalate the conflict. Keep in mind that although it may be bad to lose, total destruction should be avoided.

We stand firm when our "back is to the wall," when we are "boxed in", or when we have "no room to maneuver." These feelings can occur in psychological and physical situations. Remember that this option for managing conflict is not predicated on winning but on surviving. We can choose deceit and trickery, particularly against someone intent on harming us. We can do whatever it takes to end the conflict in a manner that prevents or reduces the possibility of harm to either party.

The guiding principles in standing firm are to avoid escalating the conflict and to respond in a way that the likelihood that you will be challenged again by the same person is diminished. For example, students may feel teachers have backed them into a corner and that they have no choice but to stand firm. Teachers may feel that parents or administrators have created situations that leave them no choice but to stand firm. As teachers, it is important that we do not force students into feeling that they have no options. Also, when we are the one being attacked, we should be aware of our options. We should stand firm only when other options are impractical or dangerous.

Rules for Standing Firm

We suggest that standing firm should be low on your priority of conflict management responses. However, you may be confronted with a situation in which this option is your *only* choice. If this occurs, it is important to respond in a way that terminates conflict with minimal damage, reduces opportunity for retribution, and maintains your rights. How? First, whenever possible, avoid confrontation with anyone who has nothing to lose. The basis for this principle lies in the fact that conflicts occurring within controlled environments are potentially less damaging than those in uncontrolled or unpredictable circumstances. For instance, if you are accosted in a professional environment, an element of control is present within the setting. Informal "rules" probably will restrict the conflict to a verbal exchange, even though it may be heated. By contrast, if you are accosted in a dark alley, the "rules" for interaction may be unknown. You may be involved with an individual who does not care about what she or he does, how it is done, or the consequences. When faced with this situation, you cannot rely on informally learned societal rules (contracts) for decency. Your attacker has nothing to lose. Consequently, he or she will not act in a prescribed manner and you will be in a highly threatening position. Of course, it is probably better not to walk down dark alleys in the first place.

Second, remember, your goal is restoration of harmony, not to win (Bolton, 1979). Therefore, if you have to respond, use minimum force, verbal or physical, to restore harmony. Following this rule indicates to the other person that your goal is managing conflict, not winning. Also, following this rule establishes a sense of fairness that can reduce the potential for later vengeful acts or retribution by the other person.

Third, if you are forced to stand firm, never extend your reaction to the other person beyond your ability to return to a balanced position. If you are verbally attacked and must choose to respond, your verbal response should be specific to the attack. It should avoid other issues of contention like historical data about other conflicts with that person. By keeping the focus on the moment, you increase the possibility of finding a way to manage the present issue, limit the number of issues to be addressed, reduce the amount of information that might be contended, and in the long run, reduce the possibility of a further attack to your response (Johnson & Johnson, 1991). For example, consider the following interchange between a teacher and a student:

AMY: I don't think you treat me fairly.

TEACHER: What do you mean?

AMY: You always pick on me.

T: How do I pick on you?

AMY: You embarrass me when I don't have the right answer in class.

T: You never do your homework, you don't come to class prepared, you always are talking to your neighbors, you don't behave yourself in class, and you say I am picking on you!

In this interchange, the teacher might be very frustrated, feel challenged, and be correct in the litany of observations made in his or her final statement. However, this response moves the discussion away from the presenting issue of fair treatment. The teacher's final statement expands discussion to the student's behavior, provides the student many opportunities for counterargument, and sets the stage for an expanded altercation instead of moving the discussion toward resolution of the student's original assertion. The teacher's final statement extended beyond what would be an appropriate response. The response would increase hostility and conflict, not reduce it.

Is this the right time and place to stand firm? Usually, when you first come under attack, you are in the worst position to respond effectively. Therefore, the first rule is to buy time and gain distance from the attack. If this means that you should retreat, then retreat. If your back is to the wall, then you have to calm yourself and take control of your fighting instinct to provide yourself mental and emotional space to maneuver. Your calmness will tend to reduce tension in your opponent. Your disengagement will tend to break the negative bond your opponent has established. In boxing, fighters are told to stay out of the corner and stay off the ropes. Also, they are cautioned to stay in the center of the ring and keep moving. This strategy can be helpful in all conflict situations. By gaining time and distance, you can avoid being trapped in an indefensible position, and like a boxer in the ring, you will have a greater chance of avoiding a "knockout." Stand firm with a clear mind so that you can better dictate the time and place of interaction.

How to Stand Firm

1. If you are forced into a situation where the only choice open to you is standing firm, then respond in a way that uses the previous admonitions and incorporates the following tenets.

2.   Physically stand your ground by making good eye contact. Square your body to the attacker. Center yourself, both physically and emotionally. Be aware of your surroundings. Be open to all inputs from the outside. Shut off your internal self talk so that you can attend to what is "coming at you."

3.   Take control of the situation by being specific with your comments. In a verbal interchange, respond calmly and thoughtfully to what is presented. Focus on the underlying meaning of what is said. Avoid being caught up in side issues or nonissues.

4.   Move toward harmony. To do this, acknowledge that a problem exists. Enlist the other party to join you in focusing on possible solutions to the problem. For instance, the following exemplifies this approach: "I can see that there is a problem. I am wondering what we could do to resolve it?"

5.   Physically and psychologically "disengage." This helps break the tension and establishes an atmosphere of mutual problem solving. To "disengage," you must maintain a perspective that focuses on the issue and not on how you feel. Your ability to manage conflict is directly proportional to your ability to keep focus on the external problem, not on your internal dynamics.

EXAMPLE

Conflict: Between two teachers

The problem: A mathematics teacher who in following the new state guidelines to incorporate a problem-solving focus is challenged by another mathematics teacher that his approach does not sufficiently nurture students.

The standing firm approach: The mathematics teacher is firmly convinced that the problem-solving approach being recommended by the state guidelines and applied in his classroom is currently the best possible approach to math education. Although he believes that nurturing is important, he does not believe that this should be the primary requirement of good teaching. Rather, he believes that helping students develop skills that will last beyond the classroom and the ability to act responsibly is more important. Therefore, he stands firm and states that he will continue to use his approach to teaching.

FACILITATIVE STRATEGIES

Problem Solving

When to Use Problem Solving

The problem-solving approach is applicable when one places equal weight on maintaining interpersonal relationships and achieving goals (Blake, Shepard, & Mouton,

1964; Hamilton et al., 1982). If conflict is to be embraced in an open, caring environment, then this is an acceptable approach.

Rules for Using Problem Solving

Rules for effective use of the problem-solving approach have been offered by a number of authors (Hamilton et al., 1982; Blake et al., 1964). Bolton (1979), in his discussion of this approach, captures the essential rules of operation offered by others:

1. **Define** the problem in terms of *needs*, not solutions.
2. **Brainstorm** possible solutions.
3. **Select** the solution(s) that will best meet both parties' needs and **check possible consequences**.
4. **Plan** who will do what, where, and by when.
5. **Implement** the plan.
6. **Evaluate** the problem-solving process and, at a later date, how well the solution turned out. (p. 240)

How to Use Problem Solving

Problem solving can be an effective conflict management approach. It is most effective when users openly share their concerns; identify basic needs, wants, issues, and possible solutions; attempt to reach consensus agreement; and mesh their insights to arrive at mutually agreeable solutions.

EXAMPLE

Conflict: Between student and classroom atmosphere

The problem: A student from a nonwhite minority group feels isolated in an all-white classroom. The teacher becomes aware of this and attempts to find a way to help the student.

The problem-solving approach: The teacher meets with the school counselor and a curriculum expert to discuss possible strategies and/or activities that could help the student feel more comfortable in the classroom.

Negotiating

When to Negotiate

Whenever you enter a no-win, zero-sum game, you are in a conflict situation. In this type of situation, the conflict becomes a "winner-loser contest." If your adversary is unwilling or unable to change his or her perception of the situation and continues to see it as an all-or-nothing situation, then you are forced into a binary situation, either you win or you lose. Negotiating is a means of broadening your options beyond these two choices. It provides an opportunity to achieve a portion of your goals while allowing your adversary the same possibility (Dobson & Miller, 1974; Hamilton et al., 1982; Johnson & Johnson, 1991).

Rules for Negotiating

Teachers can serve as a positive model for conflict-managing behavior by responding appropriately in conflict situations. This can be demonstrated in using negotiating to manage conflict. For instance, by avoiding personal gain when it is at the expense of the other person, teachers demonstrate a willingness to act fairly and with sensitivity to others' needs. This attitude of fairness is the basis for the following rules for negotiating:

- Provide all parties an opportunity to identify and label their feelings about the conflict situation.
- Ask all involved individuals to identify what they are willing to do and/or give up to reduce conflict and what they want from the process.
- Develop, accept, implement, and evaluate an action plan that is mutually agreeable to all parties.

Is it the right time and place for negotiating? Is there undue pressure to act quickly? In many situations, the need for an immediate action does not allow adequate time to negotiate. Therefore, although timing is important, the initial goal might be to lower the negatively charged emotional atmosphere so "reason can prevail." Frequently, a better atmosphere for negotiation can be created by letting time pass, calming the atmosphere, and finding ways to delay premature action. Once a proper atmosphere has been created, negotiation can begin.

How to Negotiate

Negotiation depends on compromise. More specifically, both parties have to be willing to participate in a process in which they share their needs, state their wants, and creatively contribute to ways that they can achieve a portion of their goals while helping their adversary do likewise. To accomplish this end, both parties must learn to relax, trust the process, listen to the others' ideas, and be open to possible resolutions to the conflict. Specific strategies that are helpful include the following:

- Get agreement from all parties that they will consider all possibilities.
- Work at keeping everyone's thinking simple and focused. Help individuals to avoid getting caught up in side issues, false issues, or nonissues.
- Despite your best efforts, individuals may be unwilling or unable to compromise. Be aware that this may happen, and, if necessary, use another conflict-reducing option.

EXAMPLE

Conflict: Between teacher and counselor

The problem: A school counselor would like to take students from an English teacher's classroom every Tuesday for 8 weeks to participate in a self-esteem enhancement program.

The negotiating approach: The teacher believes that the students could benefit from the counselor's program but that they cannot afford to miss 20% of their available class time. Consequently, she initiates a conversation with the counselor to negotiate the amount of time students will miss her class.

Confluent Response

The confluent response has several elements.

1. Recognizing feelings directly
2. Expressing feelings and observations honestly
3. Making transitions to problem solving

For example:

> TEACHER: You're both very angry.
>
> SAM: You're darn right I am.
>
> SUSIE: You'd be mad too if you had to put up with his stupidity all day. Who cares?
>
> TEACHER: Well, you can continue to yell at each other or talk about what is making each of you mad. Since we teachers are big on talking, I'd prefer you talk about what each of you did that makes the other mad. You also might tell me why you think fighting will make you feel better. What do you say?

When to Use Confluence

The confluent response is appropriate in most conflict situations (Blake et al., 1964; Dobson & Miller, 1974; Hamilton et al., 1982; Weeks, 1992). It is the one strategy most likely to move toward restoring harmony and therefore should be used first. Only when it is not effective should other choices be considered.

Rules for the Confluent Response

- Center yourself. Slow yourself mentally and physically.
- Acknowledge students' right to have the feelings that they do.

- Express your feelings and observations.
- Help students make a transition to problem solving.
- Engage in problem solving to attempt to meet all students' needs.

How to Use the Confluent Response

Most classroom situations lend themselves to using the confluent strategy. However, there has to be an adequate amount of time to help students problem-solve. This may be difficult in a typical classroom situation. An effective alternate is to end overt conflict as soon as possible by acknowledging the conflict and students' desire to deal with it. Once overt conflict has been reduced, problem-solving time should be scheduled for leading combatants through the problem-solving process.

- Acknowledge students' right to feel whatever they feel.
- Help redirect mutual attacks. Focus on central issues.
- Harmonize by helping combatants problem-solve to mutually satisfying goals.

EXAMPLE

Conflict: Between two students, with teacher as facilitator

The problem: A student has to work with another student whom he does not like.

The confluent approach: The teacher says to the student, "I can understand how it might be difficult to feel as comfortable with everyone as you might like, but it is helpful to learn to work with different individuals." Then the teacher describes what can be gained from such an interaction and how she might facilitate the process. This approach follows the basic principles of the confluent approach (i.e., awareness, acknowledgment, blending, and leading).

While each of these strategies can be effective and each has a set of rules and steps to use, the most important aspect is to estimate the situation. Estimating the situation provides the data necessary to choose which strategy to use to move toward harmony.

ANOTHER LOOK AT THE EXAMPLE FROM CHAPTER 1

It is Parents' Night at School in early October. A sixth-grade teacher, Mr. Rich, begins to address a room full of parents, when a parent stands up and begins to criticize him because of his teaching style and classroom organization. It is obvious that the parent speaking is very upset and the criticism revolves around modern methods that Mr. Rich has been using. The parent wants Mr. Rich to return to the basics and stop the fancy stuff. It also is obvious to Mr. Rich, by noticing the head nods of other parents, that others share similar feelings and ideas. Other parents remain silent or seem to be embarrassed by the particular parent's outburst.

If you were Mr. Rich, what would you do?

Each response here relates to strategies outlined in this chapter:

- Remain silent until the parent was done and then continue with your prepared presentation. (**Doing nothing**)
- Become flustered and leave the room. (**Withdrawing**)
- Tell the parent that he is correct and that a change will be made. (**Smoothing**)
- Change the subject to something else. (**Diversion**)
- Ask the parent to be more explicit about his feelings so that your understanding of them can be used for arriving at a mutually satisfying solution. (**Confronting**)
- Tell the parent that you are the expert and you will run the classroom the way you see fit. (**Forcing**)
- Begin explaining your philosophy of teaching and education. (**Standing firm**)
- Attempt to determine specific aspects of the parent's complaint so that possible solutions can be reached. (**Problem solving**)
- Try to negotiate with the complaining parent and others about how to run the classroom. (**Negotiating**)
- Acknowledge the parent's right to feel and think that way and begin a discussion among those in attendance concerning the remarks of the complaining parent. (**Confluent response**)

SUMMARY

In this chapter, we have advanced the belief that individuals in higher-status positions, notably teachers, should accept the responsibility for establishing a positive attitude characterized by respect and caring and that this attitude can provide the foundation for facilitative conflict management. In addition to general conflict management approaches of denial, avoidance, capitulation, domination, bargaining, and applying a "Band-Aid," we presented 10 specific options for managing conflict. We described four passive approaches: doing nothing, withdrawing, smoothing, and using diversion. We then discussed three assertive approaches: confronting, forcing, and standing firm. Finally, we presented three facilitative approaches: problem solving, negotiating, and the confluent response. In addition, the chapter focused on when to use each strategy, rules for using each, how to use each, and an example applying the strategy in a school setting.

Each option has its value. All have specific times and circumstances when they are best. In general, the best option in most situations is the confluent response. This option takes into account needs of involved parties and uses problem solving to arrive at the most harmonious conclusion. By contrast, the option that should be used sparingly, usually as a last resort, is the forcing approach.

Finally, we noted that, with the exception of the forcing strategy, these conflict-managing strategies are built on the assumption that restoration of harmony in relationships is the primary goal, not winning.

REFERENCES

Blake, R. R., Shepard, H. A., & Mouton, J. S. (1964). *Managing intergroup conflict in industry*. Houston, TX: Gulf.

Bolton, R. (1979). *People skills*. Upper Saddle River, NJ: Prentice Hall.

Cialdini, R. B. (1988). *Influence: Science and practice* (2nd ed.). New York: HarperCollins.

Dobson, T., & Miller, V.J. (1974). *Giving in to get your way*. New York: Delacourt.

Hamilton, C., Parker, C., & Smith, D. D. (1982). *Communicating for results*. Belmont, CA: Wadsworth.

Johnson, D. W., & Johnson, F. P. (1991). *Joining together* (4th. ed.). Upper Saddle River, NJ: Prentice Hall.

Lee, J. L., Pulvino, C. J., & Perrone, P. A. (1994). *Dynamic counseling*. Minneapolis, MN: Educational Media Corporation.

Markova, D. (1991). *The art of the possible*. Emeryville, CA: Conari.

Weeks, D. (1992). *Conflict resolution*. New York: Putnam's.

CHAPTER 6

The Confluent Response

As discussed in the previous chapter, the confluent response applies in most conflict situations. In this chapter, we will examine the confluent response in greater detail. There are several processes within the confluent response, processes emanating from the systematic practice of aikido.

The primary goal of aikido is restoration of harmony. Restoration of harmony is accomplished by using one's awareness as a basis for blending, connecting, unbalancing, and eventually leading or redirecting energy originating from an opposing force. Each step in the process provides a foundation for the subsequent step in the sequence. When taken together and systematically followed, conflict resolution can be expected.

When interpersonal conflict occurs, systematic adherence to a confluent response can lead to restoration of harmony. The five steps of the confluent response process will be presented here under the labels **awareness**, **blending**, **connecting**, **unbalancing**, and **leading**.

AWARENESS

It is obvious that if one is to interact with another in a facilitative manner, one must be aware of the other person. Awareness has proven to be most helpful when it is both general and specific, conscious, and focused. For example, when a teacher is generally aware of a student, the teacher will notice how the student communicates verbally and nonverbally, observe ways in which the student impacts others, and be cognizant of how he or she feels in the student's presence. This general awareness could lead the teacher to formulate an intuitive sense about the student and set the stage for more focused, intense personal interactions. This general awareness also can lead the teacher to closer, more specific observation and stimulate the teacher to better understand the student. This focus usually results in specific beliefs about the student, about his or her personality and interpersonal interactions. General awareness seems to provide an intuitive understanding, whereas specific awareness tests or validates initial and subsequent observations. These validated observations frequently result in established beliefs.

Discussion

This entire awareness process can occur at a subconscious level. That is, the teacher may not be cognizant of specifics of his or her observations or resulting beliefs. When this occurs, the teacher probably will respond to the student spontaneously without great forethought. Although this may be appropriate, it may lack the power of a more thoughtful, purposeful interaction. When teachers *consciously* respond to elements from their awareness, they can be more selective in what they respond to and choose specifically how they will respond.

In normal, nonspecific interactions, focused awareness usually is not important. That is, in most situations it is appropriate for teachers to be aware of students' general characteristics, attributes, or behaviors. Sometimes, however, a more focused awareness is warranted. In a classroom, for example, a teacher may be aware of the general noise, activity, or energy level and determine that all are within acceptable parameters. It also is possible that the teacher will become aware that one student in particular is noisier, more active, or more energetic than others and that this one student's actions are beyond acceptable bounds. This latter case represents **focused** awareness. It is more specific and addresses particular aspects of the student in question.

By using general and specific, conscious, and focused awareness in conflict situations, teachers can restore harmony confluently in a timely manner. For example, a teacher will be prepared to react quickly and appropriately when consciously aware of a student's general behavior, specific personality, interpersonal characteristics, and specific classroom interactions. It is harder for teachers to act as quickly or appropriately to conflict situations if they are either unaware of these dimensions or are only relatively aware at a subconscious level.

Issues

A number of factors influence a teacher's ability to be consistently aware. First, typically teachers have direct and indirect responsibility for many students. The sheer weight of numbers works against teachers' total awareness. Although they have direct responsibility for students in their classes, the classes may be too large for them to be aware of all students. Typically, in large classes teachers are more aware of unusual or demanding students and less likely to be aware of well-behaving students. Consequently, even though they have continuous contact with students, teachers may have little awareness of several students. Teachers also are indirectly responsible for students in other school settings (e.g., study halls, cafeterias, home rooms, assembly programs, field trips). Teachers may become aware of students in these indirect encounters. However, because of the intermittent nature of their contact, awareness is less likely than if students were in their classes.

Second, in addition to the pressure of numbers, teachers are under pressure from the information explosion. Teachers are constantly being asked to expand their knowledge base and to integrate new concepts or structures into their curriculum. The time needed to accomplish this is frequently taken from time that could be used to increase awareness of students.

Third, increasing diversity among students demands considerable teacher attention, thought, and action. Teachers are being expected to provide relevant education for a broad array of students with a wide spectrum of needs. This takes additional time, energy, and focus. Time taken in this regard also competes with becoming aware of students.

Finally, teachers are being expected to meet dynamically expanding teaching responsibilities. Teachers are being asked to provide education around all traditional subjects plus provide social-educational assistance in areas such as drug and alcohol abuse, suicide prevention, sexual development, and pregnancy, to name a few. The time it takes to prepare oneself and to develop programs in these areas is vast. Some of the time expended in these areas has to come from teachers' focus on individual students.

Focus

Teacher awareness of students is the basic building block of the confluent response. Without awareness, blending, connecting, unbalancing, and leading cannot occur. Although this book is not aimed specifically at reducing the pressures mentioned, increased awareness of all students can help teachers deal with conflict situations more easily and quickly. The time and energy saved can help teachers meet more challenging demands.

BLENDING

Awareness is the first step in responding confluently. The second step in this facilitative process is blending. Once a teacher is consciously aware of a conflict situation and committed to resolution, blending becomes important.

Blending is the process of joining the other person's world long enough to understand and communicate that understanding back to the person. At times this process is all that will be necessary for restoring harmony. Sometimes people just want to be heard, be understood, and have their feelings accepted as being legitimate in the situation. Even though conflict management focuses on restoring harmony as fast as possible, it is important for people to have their story heard and feel appreciated.

Discussion

Blending frequently begins by recognizing and communicating an individual's right to have and express his or her feelings. For example:

- You sound very angry. . . .
- You sound very frustrated. . . .
- You're really mad about what has happened. . . .

Although these statements begin with *you,* they focus on accepting the other person's feelings as being legitimate and appropriate. This form of "you" messages is different from the accusatory form of a you message described here:

BURT: You hurt me! *[direct blame]*

BURT: You're always doing things like that. When are you going to learn? *[historical data]*

TEACHER: I feel angry when you talk without permission. *[I message]*

TEACHER: You are talking without permission! *[you message]*

A natural next step in the blending process is to self-disclose about the conflict situation. This entails making I versus you statements. I messages are self-disclosing and responsibility taking. That is, I messages focus attention on the person making the statement. I messages are statements about your feelings and thoughts. They tell others what you feel about their behavior or an event. You messages, on the other hand, focus attention on the other person and are often accusatory or, at least, can be read that way. Very often, in conflict situations, you messages are used to blame directly or to bring up historical data.

The benefit of I messages is that your needs and feelings get known without blaming the other person(s) involved in the conflict. They divert attention away from the conflict between or among the people to you. Finally, I messages increase the likelihood that you will be understood by the other person(s).

Three different kinds of I messages are possible:

I Messages That Are Self-Disclosing

I feel like. . . .

I like. . . .

I want. . . .

I think. . . .

I'm afraid of. . . .

I Messages That Are Responsive to Situations

I did . . . because. . . .

I don't want to . . . because. . . .

I've decided . . . because. . . .

I'd like to . . . because. . . .

I Messages That Are Preventive

I need . . . because. . . .

I want . . . because. . . .

I would like to . . . because. . . .

Be careful! Just because you have *I* in a statement does not make it a true self-disclosing I message. For example:

T: I feel you mean. . . .

T: I feel you did that on purpose.

T: I think you just want to get attention.

I in front of a you message is not self-disclosing but is a veiled judgment. I messages are used only to make a transition to problem solving. Continued use of I messages can have the effect of adding to and exacerbating conflicts. No one likes to hear that her or his actions cause others a problem. Even the best-constructed I message may be the occasion for a person to feel hurt, sorry, embarrassed, or defensive.

After all, the message received is that his or her behavior is unacceptable, trouble-some, or hurtful. Sending an I message is only a transitional way of expressing your true feelings and thoughts in the situation to move on to problem solving. The I message is an expression of your right to have feelings and thoughts. After all, you have acknowledged the other person's right to have feelings and thoughts in the initial part of blending. To make an appropriate transition from your observations to I statements, you may need to refocus on the other person long enough to understand her or his point of view.

Consider this example: Jim has walked into class late for the fourth time in four days. His entry has disrupted the class.

TEACHER: *[making an I statement]* Jim, when you are late to class, it causes a problem. I have to stop whatever I'm doing. I find it distracting and I'm frustrated.

JIM: Yeah. Well, I've had a lot to do lately and sometimes I just can't get here on time.

T: *[making a transition and blending with the student]* I see. You seem to have some problems of your own lately.

JIM: Yeah! Mr. Sage asked me to help in the biology lab after fourth period. You know, getting ready for fifth period. It's a good deal for me—I learn a lot.

T: *[blending]* That sounds like a good deal for you, but. . . .

JIM: Yeah! I know it causes problems for you in this class. I did not think it was such a problem. You know, I can just slip in and get to my seat.

T: *[blending]* You sound a little surprised that it causes a problem for me or the students.

JIM: Well, not really. I can see that you have to stop and deal with my being late. You have to fill out the tardy slip and all that kind of stuff. Then I have to go the office and explain what happened. It's a hassle for you and for me.

T: *[transition to problem solving]* What do you think we can do about it?

JIM: I guess I could talk to Mr. Sage about it.

In this example, the teacher's I message established punctuation. This provided a basis for gathering information and problem solving. Blending is the momentary acknowledging and joining the other person's world as a foundation for making a transition toward problem solving and restoring harmony. In blending the teacher uses basic listening, I messages, and exploring skills to gain an understanding of the other person's perception of the situation. This includes listening to and accepting the other person's feelings.

Issues

To blend, one must be aware and have skills necessary to communicate understanding and caring. Teachers can develop and demonstrate awareness if they have sufficient time and inclination to do so. However, teachers may have to proactively develop the communication skills required in blending. This can be done through participation in workshops, professional reading, or focused learning.

Focus

The use of blending can help teachers establish understanding relationships. These relationships provide a vehicle for establishing and reaching mutual goals while providing a basis for restoration of harmony.

CONNECTING

The third phase of a confluent response is connecting. Connecting is characterized by an understanding of the other's world, respect for the individual's psychological position, commitment to forming a mutual working relationship, and active effort to involve the other person in conflict resolution. Connecting is predicated on the belief that it is possible to understand and enter another's world and, more important, that it is possible to work toward conflict resolution from within that person's world.

Discussion

Consider the following interchange:

SARGE: I think you treated me unfairly. I did all of my homework and you still gave me a failing grade.

TEACHER: I see that you did do your homework and that you did get a failing grade. It's also apparent to me that you are upset. I'm wondering, though, specifically why you are upset and why you think I treated you unfairly.

SARGE: Well, if I do my homework, I should get a good grade.

T: I see. If you do your homework, then, because you did, you should get a passing grade. Is that how you see it?

SARGE: Yes.

T: So, it's frustrating to make the effort to do the homework and not have it count toward a good grade?

SARGE: That's right. I did the homework. It should mean a good grade.

T: Thanks for being open about your concern. I can see the problem better now. It looks to me that we had two different expectations for the homework. For me, the homework was seen as a way to prepare you for the test. For you, the homework was seen as being part of the test. Do you think this is what happened?

SARGE: Well, yeah. I did think the homework was part of the test and I can see that you didn't.

T: How do you think we should handle this? Do you think we can find a way that we both could agree on?

SARGE: Probably.

T: Good.

By blending with the student and connecting with the student's world, the teacher was able to move the discussion toward mutual problem solving. To do this, the teacher had to "see" the situation as the student saw it and then use what was observed from this alternate position to move toward a mutually satisfying solution. The teacher demonstrated awareness of the student's needs, respect for the student's position, and a desire to enlist the student in finding a way to resolve the conflict.

Issues

Connecting, although important in the confluent response, can be resisted. Resistance can occur because individuals may be unsettled in their own perception, wary of letting another get too close to them, or reluctant to alter or change their thoughts or behaviors. This resistance occurs because it frequently is easier for individuals to maintain an existing condition than to face an unknown one. Consequently, a teacher who helps a student confront an alternative way of action may meet resistance. This can happen even when the student likes and respects the teacher and knows that the teacher is attempting to find a solution that is mutually satisfying. For some, change, large or small, is difficult.

Focus

Trust is a central ingredient in the connecting phase. By adapting conditions frequently discussed in counseling literature (Brammer, 1993; Corey & Corey, 1993; Okun, 1992), teachers can develop trusting relationships that will help overcome resistance and facilitate the process of connecting. By exhibiting empathy, genuineness, respect, honesty, and caring in a confidential manner, a teacher can diminish resistance to connecting and facilitate acceptance of mutual goals.

UNBALANCING

Sometimes resistance to change is strong, and normal facilitative responses fail. In these cases, the additional strategy of unbalancing may be needed. Unbalancing is a process in which one's psychological balance is taken away. When psychological balance is removed, individuals are vulnerable to change and resistance can be more easily overcome. This principle has a physical parallel in aikido. In aikido, it is easier to throw an opponent who is out of balance than one who is balanced or centered. Therefore, an aikido technique is to blend and connect with an opponent, find his or her balance point, and then unbalance the person. When this is achieved, the opponent can be thrown.

Individuals can be unbalanced psychologically in a number of ways. We will emphasize two of these: reframing and depotentiating.

Discussion

Reframing, a means for psychologically unbalancing an individual, is defined by Bandler and Grinder (1982) as "changing the frame in which a person perceives events in order to change the meaning" (p. 1). Bandler and Grinder go on to say, "When the meaning changes, the person's responses and behaviors also change" (p. 1). The following examples might add to your understanding of this definition of reframing.

One example derives from the work of Milton H. Erickson, a world-renowned hypnotherapist, who was asked by a father how to handle his daughter (Lee, Pulvino, & Perrone, 1994). He told Erickson that his daughter was strong-willed, stubborn, and unwilling to take advice. The father wanted to know what to do to control her. Erickson thought for a few minutes and then responded with something such as, "You've raised a daughter who is assertive, knows her own mind, and isn't about to go along with people just to be liked." The father thought a few minutes and then said, "Never mind!" and left (p. 117). In this example, behavior was initially viewed one way by the father, but, when reframed by Erickson, it was viewed in a totally different manner.

A second example also exemplifies reframing. As a school counselor, one of the authors was paid 10% more than teachers on the teaching salary scale because he had two professional certificates, one as a school mathematics teacher and one as a school counselor. A social worker was hired by the school district and was upset when he did not receive an additional 10% for his dual certification. He went to the school board and demanded to be paid the same as school counselors. The school board considered his request and complied. They took the 10% differential away from school counselors! The school board effectively reframed the request. Instead of seeing the request as a social worker's demand for more money, the school board *chose* to view the social worker's demand as a request for equal treatment. In doing so, they complied with the request and saved the school board money on two fronts.

How can reframing be used in exercising a confluent response? We suggest three different ways that this might be accomplished (Lee et al., 1994). First, expressed desires and feelings can be **counterbalanced**. Counterbalancing is based on the belief that student statements reflect what they want or desire. However, at times these wants or desires are expressed in a negative form. For example, a student expressing a fear of failure could be said to have a desire for success. Similarly, test anxiety could be a desire to achieve, or shyness might reflect a desire to be accepted. By counterbalancing, teachers can reframe student statements in a way that will help them see alternate possibilities.

Consider the following example in which awareness, blending, and connecting have been demonstrated by the teacher. In this example the student is talking about what is preventing her from success. Despite the teacher's positive attitude, the student is still demonstrating resistance.

TEACHER: We have been talking about this for a while, and I get the sense that you have not changed your mind. Is that true?

JULIE: I guess so.

T: Tell me specifically what seems to be the problem.

JULIE: I just get very confused when we talk.

T: I see. You have such a high desire to understand it frustrates you when you don't.

JULIE: Yes, I would like to do well.

T: Good, let's see how I can help you do that.

In this example, the teacher counterbalanced the student's statement about **confusion** with **a desire to understand**. This reframe allowed the student to view her negative statement in a positive light and opened the door for mutual problem solving.

A second way that reframing can occur is through **amplification**. Amplification pushes one's statements to the extreme. Possible solutions may be seen more clearly from this vantage point. Consider the following interchange between a student and teacher who have a solid working relationship:

BILL: I feel so guilty when I don't study.

TEACHER: You obviously don't feel guilty enough, or you would sit down and study.

BILL: You know, I guess you're right.

Because of the existing working relationship, the teacher in this example could challenge the student's statement with an amplified response. This approach could stimulate the student to look more realistically at his study habits.

A third form of reframing is to **jump to a second perspective**, a perspective that facilitates problem resolution. This form of reframing frequently helps individuals expand their awareness and consider possibilities previously unknown or unavailable to them. For example, in talking with a counselor, a client lamented that she had just lost her job. The counselor enthusiastically responded, "Great, now you can go back to school like you always wanted." The counselor heard what the client had said but chose to respond to the message from an entirely different perspective. This alternate perspective could help the client focus on the positive aspects of the job loss while avoiding getting embedded in the negative.

How can a teacher use this approach to reduce conflict? The following example in which a teacher is attempting to help one student get along with another demonstrates one way.

TEACHER: You seem to have very little patience for your partner.

KEVIN: I don't think he likes me.

T: What leads you to that conclusion?

KEVIN: He does not talk very much.

T: I see. He does not talk very much so you think that he does not like you. Could it be that he likes you but that he is shy?

KEVIN: Well, I guess so.

T: If he were shy, what would you do?

KEVIN: I'd be nice to him and give him a little more time.

T: Great! Are you willing to try that?

KEVIN: Sure.

T: Super! I'm glad you're open to the possibility. Let me know what happens.

One behavior, being withdrawn in an interpersonal interaction, can occur for many reasons. The student had been focusing on one possibility. By reframing the original information, the teacher helped the student see an alternate possibility. This reframing could lead to resolution of the student's concern.

A second way to unbalance an individual is to use the concept of **depotentiation**. Rossi (1980), in discussing Erickson's work, states that depotentiation is "a way of deautomatizing an individual's habitual modes of functioning." It is a way for opening "up the possibility that new combinations of associations and mental skills may be evolved for creative problem solving within that individual" (pp. 448–449). Viewed from another perspective, the process of depotentiation is similar to Castaneda's (1972) concept of "stopping the world": "Stopping the world is creating a certain state of 'awareness' in which reality of everyday life is altered because the flow of interpretation which ordinarily runs uninterruptedly, has been stopped by a set of circumstances alien to the flow" (p. 14).

Put simply, depotentiation is the process of altering an individual's reality. It is the process of stopping one's routine and normal patterned way of organizing information.

Albrecht (1980) presents an example that can help explain depotentiation. On the original *Tonight Show,* Doc Severinson would start the evening's entertainment by conducting the Tonight Show Band. Typically he would have his baton raised and ready as the curtain was drawn. One night, unknown to Doc, Johnny Carson had instructed the band to refrain from responding when Doc waved his baton to start the music. The curtain opened, Doc waved his baton, as he had for many previous nights, and the band players did not move. Doc became furious. He did not know what was happening, and he waved his baton faster and faster. Still no response from the band was forthcoming. Eventually he caught a glimpse of Johnny and knew that he had been set up. Later, when asked about the situation, Doc said, "It felt like somebody hit me behind the neck" (p. 37). Clearly Doc had a habitual manner of opening the show. Johnny had used band members to depotentiate or stop Doc's world. At the moment this occurred, Doc was unbalanced and open to change.

In conclusion, depotentiation serves a useful purpose when using unbalancing as part of a confluent response. It is frequently used in hypnosis (Rossi, 1980). The following example demonstrates depotentiation in a teacher—administrator verbal interaction.

A: I'm getting complaints that you are failing to provide students individual help.

T: In all classes, or in one in particular?

A: Well, mostly in your first period algebra class.

T: Do you know anything about that class?

A: Only that people are complaining.

T: I see. Maybe you should know something about it. First, as you know, it is a 50-minute class. Second, homeroom frequently cuts into that 50 minutes. Third, I have 35 students in the class. Fourth, I only have 30 desks in the class. Fifth, I've been working with the counselors to move students to other classes, and, until they do something, I've asked the custodians to get more desks. Actually, given the conditions under which I'm working, I'm surprised everyone isn't complaining. What do you plan to do to resolve the problem?

A: I don't know!

T: Well, when you do, let me know.

In this stereotypical example, the administrator had a routine or habitual way of responding to complaints (i.e., expect the teacher to change). The teacher used depotentiation to alter the administrator's reality. As a consequence of depotentiation, the administrator was "set up" to find a solution to the problem.

Issues

The act of unbalancing assumes that the person doing the unbalancing is in a position to exert power to affect or change the relationship. It is further assumed that this person will use his or her inherent power in an ethical way to benefit all involved parties.

Unbalancing through reframing and use of depotentiation is a thoughtful process. To use unbalancing effectively, individuals must be aware of specifics of situations, be cognizant of their needs, be aware of the desires of others, acknowledge environmental conditions, and exhibit creative problem-solving skills.

Focus

Unbalancing is important in the confluent response because it interferes with an individual's normal mental set, his or her attitude or belief about a situation or about an upcoming experience. This interference provides the teacher an opportunity to alter the flow of conversation, offer a different perspective, or provide alternate explanations or possibilities. Unbalancing sets the stage for leading others in conflict-reducing directions.

LEADING

Awareness, blending, connecting, and unbalancing prepare an individual to accept an alternate perspective. They establish an opening in the individual's mental set for new or different ways of responding. This opening can be filled by teachers who know how to *lead* in a conflict-reducing direction.

Discussion

In aikido, leading uses the attacking individual's energy to move the person to a position where he or she cannot hurt him- or herself or the aikido expert. Leading, in interpersonal conflict situations, is similar. It is the part of a confluent response that provides the direction or focus to the interaction. By leading, teachers can direct individuals to focus in new directions, directions that lead to conflict resolution. Consider the following interchange between a teacher and a parent:

P: I'm really upset with the way you teach mathematics.

T: Oh, what specifically is upsetting to you?

P: I don't think you spend enough time on drills.

T: I see. I can see that you think drills are important. I can understand that. I also think drills are important. I'm wondering how much time you think I spend on drills.

P: Not enough.

T: Not enough? What do you think would be enough?

P: At least 1 day per week.

T: That's interesting. I presently spend 15 minutes every day on drills. That adds up to 75 minutes a week which is one-third of the total class time. As it turns out, that is more than the 20% of class time you'd like me to spend. Maybe time isn't the issue. Could your concern be something other than the amount of time I spend on drills?

P: Well . . . my son's not doing as well as I would like in your class.

T: Yes, I know. What do you think his problem is?

In this example, the teacher used awareness of the parent's frustration to blend and connect. This was followed by consciously unbalancing the parent. Depotentiation occurred by providing specific figures that surpassed the parent's expectations for the amount of time desired and actually spent on mathematical drills. This set the stage for leading the parent to a discussion of what was more central to the conflict situation, how well her son was doing in mathematics.

Issues

Leading revolves around determining the direction that the leading will follow. Normally, leading should be focused on neutralizing an interpersonal attack. However, it may be important to do more than neutralize. On occasion, teachers may want to move interactions toward problem solving, decision making, individual responsibility taking, a particular action, or behavior change. It is important for teachers to know what they want to accomplish through the confluent response and more specifically where, why, and how they want to lead.

Focus

Leading is the final step in responding confluently. It is important in this step for teachers to have a clear idea of what is being sought. Although goal setting will be discussed in detail in the next chapter, it is important to state at this juncture that goal setting can provide teachers the target for where, how, and why they lead. By having a clear idea of what is sought, teachers can tailor their interactions with others and use confluent responses that lead to conflict resolution.

SUMMARY

A confluent response has five main aspects: awareness, blending, connecting, unbalancing, and leading. These five elements provide a basis for interaction that teachers can use to manage conflict. **Awareness** provides the knowledge of others that provides a foundation. **Blending** is a communication process that teachers can use to understand the internal state of others. **Connecting** allows teachers to be with others at a meaningful level, a level from which they can communicate understanding, caring, and respect. **Unbalancing** is a needed process that provides teachers with ways for altering individuals' mental sets so that they can provide alternate perspectives. The two major ways for unbalancing are reframing and depotentiation. Effective use of awareness, blending, connecting, and unbalancing sets the stage for teachers to **lead** individuals in directions that are consistent with goals that result in conflict management.

REFERENCES

Albrecht, K. (1980). *Brain power: Learn to improve your thinking skills*. Upper Saddle River, NJ: Prentice Hall.

Bandler, R., & Grinder, J. (1982). *Reframing*. Moab, UT: Real People Press.

Brammer, L. M. (1993). *The helping relationship* (5th ed.). Boston: Allyn & Bacon.

Castaneda, C. (1972). *Journey to Ixtlan*. New York: Simon & Schuster.

Corey, M. S., & Corey, G. (1993). *Becoming a helper* (2nd ed.). Pacific Grove, CA: Brooks/Cole.

Lee, J. L. , Pulvino, C. J., & Perrone, P. A. (1994). *Dynamic counseling* (3rd ed.). Minneapolis, MN: Educational Media.

Okun, B. F. (1992). *Effective helping* (4th ed.). Pacific Grove, CA: Brooks/Cole.

Rossi, E. L. (Ed.) (1980). *The nature of hypnosis and suggestion*. Vol. 1. New York: Irvington.

CHAPTER 7

Conflict Management:
A Solution-Oriented Perspective

In this chapter, we adapt principles of solution-oriented counseling to conflict management. For more information about these concepts, refer to the additional resources listed at the end of this chapter.

Solution-oriented counseling focuses on solutions rather than causes of problems. The emphasis in solution-oriented counseling is on effecting change in the present with minimal concern for past events. We believe that a similar approach can be taken for managing conflict. By understanding individuals, their needs, and environmental interactions, teachers can anticipate potential conflict-producing situations. Accurate anticipation can lead to preparation and timely action. The result of this action will be management of conflict.

This chapter has six sections. In the first, we discuss issues of social responsibility and discuss how failure to accept this responsibility plays a part in fostering conflict. We then turn our attention to finding exceptions to conflict situations. Third, we consider the value of goal setting in conflict management. The value of adopting a future orientation is discussed next. Fifth, we describe three ways that teachers can involve others in managing conflict. Finally, we adapt the problem-solving model Time Zero to conflict management in the schools.

SOCIAL RESPONSIBILITY

A school is a social organization in which participants (e.g., students, teachers, administrators, staff) must interact in socially acceptable ways to achieve educational goals. When all parties abide by implicit and explicit rules of conduct, a functional community of learning is likely to result. However, when any individual fails to abide by these rules, learning is inhibited and conflict is promoted. Teachers can play a central part in assuring learning and inhibiting conflict by being aware of how broken contracts affect individual behavior and not following through on commitments contributes to conflict. A brief discussion of each follows.

Contracts

The concept of contracts has been discussed in Chapter 2. By way of review, when contracts, formal and informal agreements between or within individuals, are broken, conflict is likely to occur. Teachers can help prevent this occurrence by using confluent responses to confront individuals who they believe are breaking contracts to themselves or others. By making explicit others' contract-breaking behavior, teachers can inhibit negative behavior while producing a foundation for positive action.

Consider the following dialogue as a positive example of this type of teacher interaction. In this example, the teacher had asked John to see her after class. The following interchange took place:

TEACHER: John, when we talked last Monday, you told me that I could expect you to take your small-group project seriously.

JOHN: That's true.

T: Since we talked, I have been impressed with how you have worked—that is, up to today. Today, I believe you slipped back to old behaviors.

JOHN: I know.

T: What happened?

JOHN: I don't know. I just couldn't get into it today.

T: What was different today?

JOHN: I just think I didn't push myself today.

T: What do you think I should do about that?

JOHN: Give me another chance.

T: Let's suppose I do give you another chance. What could I expect to see?

JOHN: I'll be serious. I won't act up.

T: That sounds good. What should I do if you slip again?

JOHN: I won't. But, if I do, then call my parents. They'll probably ground me.

T: OK. I'll give you a chance. If you stick to our agreement, I won't do anything. If you don't, I'll call your parents. Agreed?

JOHN: Agreed. By the way, thanks.

T: You're welcome.

The teacher had a contract with John, and John had a contract with himself. The teacher was afraid of what John's broken contracts would mean to John and possibly to his small-group activity. The teacher confronted John with his breaking of both contracts, discussed the consequences of broken contracts, and established the basis for a new contract. The discussion was done in a helpful, confidential, timely, and yet confrontational manner. In doing so, the teacher encouraged an immediate change in John's behavior (present-time action), inhibited development of additional conflict, and forced John into contract-abiding behavior.

Consequences of Behavior

It is generally accepted that individuals meet many of their personal needs through interpersonal interactions (Maslow, 1969). In most situations, interpersonal interactions that occur are positive. However, in some cases they are negative. Some individuals either are unaware of their impact on others or are aware but uncaring. When either attitude is manifest, conflict is likely to result. Teachers can provide a positive force, foster learning, inhibit the development of conflict, and encourage social responsibility. They can do so by confronting individuals with an external view of their behavior and by helping them see potential consequences of their actions.

Consider the following example in which a supervising classroom teacher is discussing classroom behavior with her student teacher:

TEACHER: In observing you today, I was aware of many things you do well and one in particular that I think you might want to work on. Which would you like to discuss first?

PRACTICE TEACHER: Is this a good news/bad news thing?

T: I think so.

PT: OK. Let's discuss the bad news first.

T: OK. Let me start by saying that discipline is an important part of classroom management. Through our discussions and my observation of you in the classroom, I believe that you are aware of this. However, the way you are going about maintaining discipline is problematic.

PT: Is there something specific you've noticed?

T: To maintain discipline, you seem to have adapted a condescending attitude toward students. For example, if a student asks a question that you think has little merit, you tend to respond sarcastically rather than address the question. This type of response may quiet students but also could convey undue negativity.

PT: What do you mean?

T: Students don't want to be put down. Nor should they be. When they are, the shy ones will withdraw and not participate. The more aggressive students will find ways to get back at you. In either case, you will have been responsible for establishing a classroom atmosphere that will impede learning. You and the students will be the losers.

PT: I wasn't aware I was doing this. I am aware that I get irritated with dumb questions. What would be a better way to respond?

T: Occasionally you will get dumb questions, at least dumb to you. Remember though, the question may not feel dumb to the student that is asking it. What can you do? First, take time to compose yourself. Then, acknowledge the question and the student who asks it. Finally, answer the question.

PT: Thanks. I'll work on responding more positively. Now, what's the good news?

T: The good news is that in teaching the class you demonstrated great organization of your material, your multimedia presentation was superb, and, in general, you were very responsive to students.

PT: Well, thank you.

T: You're welcome.

Conflict in schools can arise at many levels. The supervising teacher in this example was aware of the conflict that could occur if the student teacher continued to respond sarcastically to students. The teacher helped the student teacher become aware of personal behavior that was in his blind zone, a zone in which he did not know what he was doing or only knew at a subconscious level. By confronting the student teacher with his behavior, the teacher brought materials from the student teacher's blind zone out into the open (Luft, 1969). This approach provided an opportunity for learning and growth. Also, by confronting the student teacher with potential consequences of his behavior, the supervising teacher reduced the possibility of conflict.

Commitment

The importance of meeting implicit or explicit contractual agreements and being aware of consequences of one's behavior was discussed earlier. In addition to these considerations, teachers can foster social responsibility by soliciting and encouraging commitment to action. More specifically, teachers can help others move toward action by strategically using **reporter**-type questions of Who? What? Where? When? Why? and How? Through use of these questions, teachers can help others clarify what they believe needs to be done and move them toward initiating action. The following interchange between a teacher and school counselor demonstrates this approach:

TEACHER: I'd like to follow up on what is being done in Mark's case.

COUNSELOR: Sure. What would you like to know?

T: Well, the last time we talked I shared my frustration about Mark's behavior in class. I'm concerned for him and for the class. What have you done so far?

C: I've talked with Mark. I've also called and talked with his parents.

T: What else do you plan to do?

C: I'd also plan to talk with his other teachers.

T: That sounds like a good idea. When will you do that?

C: I should be able to get to everyone before the end of the week.

T: Once you've talked with everyone, what will you do?

C: I'll integrate what I hear from all of these sources, then I'll set up a meeting with you, Mark, and myself to discuss what needs to be done next.

T: When do you think that meeting can occur?

C: By Tuesday of next week at the latest.

T: Good. Will you involve Mark's parents any further?

C: I will if the three of us can't make sufficient progress toward resolving the problem.

T: OK. I feel better knowing that you are working on this. Thanks.

C: Sure. I'll keep you informed.

In this example, the teacher used reporter questions to stay informed about action being taken in regard to one of his students. The questions asked by the teacher also could be viewed as being motivating stimulants for continued action by the school counselor. More specifically, by using "when" questions, the teacher inferred that he expected action to be taken in a timely manner. The school counselor was sufficiently motivated and responded appropriately.

In conclusion, teachers can help prevent or manage conflict by helping others be aware of their contractual obligations and consequences of their actions. Teachers also can help individuals follow through on their commitments by using reporter-type questions to focus their attention and to stimulate them to action. Through the careful use of these processes, teachers can help others achieve social responsibility.

FINDING EXCEPTIONS

When people become involved in a conflict situation, they focus on the conflict, their negative feelings, and their own immediate needs. When this happens, people have a tendency to focus on negatives and become **historians**. For example:

- You always. . . .
- You have never. . . .
- Last week you. . . .
- Ever since we . . . you. . . .

The very process of defining a conflict situation or defining things in absolute historical ways implies that at times what is being described does *not* occur, that exceptions to the conflict situation exist. As a mediator in a conflict situation, you may often find it useful to help identify exceptions to the situation that is occurring. Reminding people of exceptions can help resolve conflicts in the present. An example may help in understanding this principle.

Best friends probably use *always* when they fight more than when they disagree with others. The reason we use the term *always* when fighting is that it increases the power of what we say. The student being attacked responds to *always,* and the level of conflict and extent of accusations dramatically increase. The precipitating factor in the conflict is quickly lost, and soon *always* is applied to a host of other interactions.

When faced with a situation such as this, teachers should attempt to get combatants' attention. This will keep the emotional fire from spreading. A simple "Whoa" along with an enforced time in which there cannot be a direct exchange between individuals might be warranted. If dealing with students who can write, have them write down what they think and feel, what their intentions were, and how they feel about what has happened.

Hopefully, this process will provide a cooling-off period, give you insight into what is happening, take fuel out of the conflict, and get combatants ready to find exceptions. Ask each of them to describe one time in their relationship when they were able to disagree without getting into a fight. Now the $64,000 question: Do they want to end their friendship, just keep fighting, or work things out as they have in the past?

If they choose to fight, you might suggest some game in which they have equal skills (sort of like a joust). If they choose to end their friendship, that is their decision—for now. If they choose to work things out like they have in the past, stay with them and help them through the working-out process. Frequently, all you will have to do is to keep them focused on the issue at hand and provide a consistently even emotional force.

Helping students involved in a conflict situation to identify positive exceptions to their present interaction promotes positive feelings, thoughts, and actions. This process is a potentially powerful way of mediating conflict situations.

GOAL SETTING

Setting goals in a conflict situation is only applicable when individuals are committed to working toward achieving individual or mutual needs. However, sometimes one individual in the conflict will ask the teacher to help settle differences and set mutually agreeable goals for dealing with the conflict. For example, a student may ask a teacher to intervene to stop other students from picking on him. The implication is that the teacher should in some way control the other students' behavior.

Setting goals is the pivotal process in conflict management. Once teachers have blended and developed a basic understanding of the conflict situation and then reframed any negative feelings, fears, or anxieties, goals can be established. Effective conflict management requires focusing on future action.

We recommend using an open-ended question similar to one of the following when setting goals:

- What do you want to be different when this situation is done?
- What would you want to be different if the conflict went away?
- What were you trying to achieve?
- What are you trying to accomplish here?

Further sessions with the same student(s) might be initiated with an open-ended question similar to one of these:

- What was the goal we set the last time we met?
- Have your goals changed since the last time we met?

These questions are open-ended while focusing on behavior and the future.

In the following discussion, we stress action. The emphasis on action is central to effective conflict management. We believe goals should focus on those things that are under an individual's control (e.g., his or her behavior and focus).

Goals are under the person's control. When students ask teachers for conflict mediation, the students' initial goal statement frequently is aimed at having another student change, ridding themselves of some feeling or fear, or achieving a desired or future psychological state—none of which are directly controllable. For example:

- I wish I were more motivated, then Mr. Lee would leave me alone.
- I want Tom to get off my back.
- I want people to like me better; I want to be more popular.
- If I were only smarter, things would be a lot better. The other kids wouldn't make fun of me.
- I could learn to use a computer a lot better if John weren't such a jerk.

None of these goal statements are within the student's direct control. Feelings, fears, anxieties, and thoughts are not *directly* controllable. Motivation, feeling better, and other psychological qualities are not attainable by sheer will power. If they were, few people would have emotional, psychological, or behavioral problems. At the same time, other students' actions are even less directly controllable except through coercion, which causes additional conflict. If teachers accept these kind of goal statements, mediation is doomed to failure.

Effective goals specify what students will be doing when on track toward achieving their goals. This is far different than teachers specifying what the student(s) will be doing. For example:

- We will have a 6-week self-concept development group for those who are having difficulty making friends.
- I will use a behavioral approach to help John learn better conflict management skills.
- In our peer mediation program, teachers will spend 3 days training mediators.

These examples tell us what the teacher(s) will be doing but only imply how students will either be psychologically different or act differently. Effective goal statements specify what the student(s) will be doing when they are on track to achieving goals and managing conflict. Some well-formed student-stated goals are as follows:

- I will study during my Tuesday and Thursday study periods rather than talk with John.
- When I feel angry and want to hit someone, I will ask to go to the counselor's office for a time-out.
- I will spend time playing John's favorite game at least three times this week rather than insisting on playing only the games I want.

Notice that these goal statements all specify student behaviors when they are on track to avoiding conflict situations. The actions are under the students' control and do not depend on other people changing, a shift in feelings, or some future psychological state.

Effective goal statements specify conditions under which action can be observed. Goal statements detail a specific place in which goal actions are expected to occur, usually related to where the conflict occurs (e.g., the playground, classroom, hallway, media center). This guideline allows anyone in those places, in addition to the student(s), to report on goal-related actions. It also implies that meaningful goals are stated relative to specific contexts, which helps guard against stating goals in universal and perfectionistic terms. The previous examples specify time, place, and circumstances.

Effective goal statements may specify actions, in percentages, degrees, or numbers, that will be acceptable during a specific time period. In several of the prior goal statements, a specification is included of the frequency of actions expected as part of the goal (e.g., playing someone else's game at least *twice* a week). It is important to keep in mind both positive and negative effects of contracts. Remember, when contracts are not fulfilled, they leave negative residual effects. Residual effects can be psychological (e.g., a lower self-concept, lower self-esteem, fewer feelings of self-efficacy). These can be accompanied by feelings of guilt because the person did not live up to the contracts. The residual effects also may be physical, as when students have physical stress reactions to conflict situations.

On the positive side, when contracts are completed, there are the positive side effects of raised self-concept, higher self-esteem, greater feelings of self-efficacy, and feelings of pride. Positive physical side effects also emerge. When people fulfill their contracts, they usually have less sickness and fewer of the physical reactions associated with stress.

We believe that self-concepts and self-esteem can be raised through positive action. Making positive self-statements and focusing on feeling better about oneself have a momentarily positive effect on self-concepts and self-esteem. By contrast, positive, successful action, completing implicit and explicit contracts, are primary ways for developing long-term positive self-concepts and heightened self-esteem.

Goals are contracts between teachers and students and contracts that students make with themselves and one another. A key in setting goals is to specify conditions in such a way that if the goal is unfulfilled, the student will still be able to save face. Second, the percentage, degree, or number of actions must be realistic. This usually means that goals should not be stated as universals or absolutes, such as these:

- I'll never pick on Jane again.
- I'll never act up in English class again.

It is natural to make mistakes and experience temporary failures. Very few people are perfect! Remember that expecting perfection, when unrealistic, can lead to an internal state of conflict.

Some circumstances are beyond our control that may make universal or absolute goals unattainable. Sometimes "The dog chewed up my homework!" is literally a true account of what occurred. One of the authors had a graduate student who came to the last class, when the semester term paper was due, with a power cord full of teeth marks. The student reported that her pet rabbit had chewed on her computer cord and had caused a short circuit. The electrical short circuit had fried her hard disk, and she had lost the paper she was scheduled to turn in that day. She asked for an extension because of extenuating circumstances beyond her control. Her extension was granted. Nobody could make up that excuse!

Managing conflicts means that the number of conflicts are reduced and that the explosiveness of combatants' reaction to inevitable conflicts is lessened. Thus, an initial goal negotiated between two combatants who fight nearly everyday, such as a brother and sister, might read like the following:

Week 1: At least once each day when I get mad at Sam/Mary, I will write down the following without saying a word and give my note to my father/mother. I will write down the day and time, what set me off, how I felt, and what I wanted to say but did not.

Week 2: At least once a day when I get mad at Sam/Mary, I will write down the following without saying a word and give my note to my father/mother. I will write down the day and time, what set me off, how I felt, what I wanted to say and did not, and what I could have said that would have made things better.

During subsequent weeks, the number of notes per day can be increased, and/or a "prize" might be added for times that combatants come up with the identical written solutions. Eventually the contract can go from writing to talking—again, a parent should be monitoring the process and progress. A teacher can use the same approach in the classroom with students who experience verbal and/or physical conflict.

Effective goals are stated in a positive form. When goals are stated in a negative way, the danger arises of creating the very thing that is to be avoided. For example:

- I won't make smart remarks to Kathy anymore.
- I won't be late with my report next week.

Both examples are stated in the negative. Negative injunctions tend to be recursive and produce themselves. When students try not to think of smart remarks, the focus of attention is on smart remarks, which increases the likelihood of thinking about smart remarks! Students then must resist temptation to use them. Thinking about not being late focuses attention on being late, the very thing the student is trying to avoid. Remember, where we focus our attention tends to produce conditioned feelings and behavior. It is far more productive to form goals in the positive form:

- I will say nice things to Kathy.
- I'll get to class on time.

Effective goals are stated in the students' language. If students are to have a commitment to goals, they must identify with them. Identification can be increased if students' goals are stated in their language rather than in the teacher's language. Actually, it is preferable to have students write their goals with your guidance so that words are theirs and the intent is consistent with concepts that we have been discussing. Here is a comparison of student talk with teacher talk:

Student Language	**Psychological/Teacher Language**
I'll get along better with the other kids.	I'll communicate better with the other children.
I'll do my homework.	I'll complete my assignments.

I'll stay in my seat.   I'll behave appropriately in class.
I'll study more.   I'll commit more time to studying.

Individuals in conflict must understand the situation and have commitment to established goals. Both of these elements, understanding and commitment, can be enhanced by having involved individuals state goals in their own terms.

A Summary Example

An example follows that reflects the concepts discussed to this point. This example is drawn from an extreme situation that has been occurring in a number of Japanese middle schools. It appears that an entire class can exercise so much pressure that students are driven to commit suicide. Pressure typically is applied to students who are academically talented, lack social skills, and are nonathletic.

To understand how this might happen, it is helpful to recognize that Japanese schools are extremely competitive. Academically talented students who do not endear themselves to their peers by socializing or participating in athletics pose a threat to the entire class. The taunting of students who fit this description can be vicious and unrelenting. With this extreme situation as a point of comparison, what might a teacher do with a class that makes one student a scapegoat for others' fear of rejection, competitiveness, or fear of failure? To answer this question, we could look to positive, counterbalancing desires and feelings as a source for establishing goals.

The teacher would have at least three possibilities for intervention. She could attempt to help the student who was being singled out, try to alter the social behavior of the group, or attempt some combination of these two approaches. For purposes of discussion, let us assume the teacher chooses to affect the total group. What might be done that would be consistent with our previous discussion about counterbalancing and goal setting?

First, the teacher would have to identify counterbalancing forces for each of the groups' identified characteristics. She might determine that the counterbalancing force for being rejected is the desire to be accepted; for competitiveness, fear of being cooperative; and for fear of failure, desire to succeed. Second, the teacher might focus on goal setting. After determining counterbalancing forces, she could help class members establish goals consistent with these desires. The creation of work groups, recreational groups, or focus groups could establish opportunities for students to develop relationships. This strategy would remove, or at least dilute, feelings of isolation and rejection. These groups could have an added benefit. As students participated in groups, they would learn the value of cooperation, which would help reduce the competitiveness previously experienced. Finally, the teacher could create situations in which students experienced success, experiences that provided them an opportunity for constructive feedback. This might be accomplished initially by reducing expectations, providing additional tutelage, or involving significant others in their education. Once students learned that they could be successful, educational expectations could be adjusted to be commensurate with their psychological comfort level.

FUTURE PACING

Future pacing can be used to help students project into the future consequences of their present actions. This process encourages students to envision future occurrences of conflict situations and how they can be dealt with. Further, it encourages students to anticipate ways to address occurrences *before they happen*. Statements like the following are useful for stimulating focus on the future:

- How will you keep these actions going?
- What will you do differently in the future to keep it from happening again?
- Can you see yourself using this solution again in the future? How?
- Tell me how you plan to apply what we've discussed in the next week or so.
- I'd be interested in knowing how what we have discussed is going to make a difference tomorrow.
- I'm pleased you have found something that might help. How are you going to apply it?

Statements of this type also can be used to motivate students. By extending the negative conflict situation into the future, students can be helped to understand difficulties that they will face if they do not take positive action.

- How much longer do you think you can hide your feelings?
- If you continue to act this way, what effect will it have on your future?
- What will happen if you get in twice as many fights every day?

The focus of discussions is on the future and change. All future pacing assumes that the future will be different. Future pacing invites students to discuss how they will make *positive* changes occur and what they will do to continue their movement toward a state of harmony.

An Example

A senior in a computer class continually was disruptive. Yet, he continuously talked about his primary ambition in life: to work with computers in a major software development firm. The student did not see a connection between his ongoing behavior and his stated ambition. The student's teacher was aware of the student's behavior and stated ambitions. She thought that he might benefit from future pacing and decided to have a conversation with him.

TEACHER: Mark, I heard you say that you would like to work in a computer firm after graduation.

MARK: Yes, I would.

T: I'm wondering what will happen on the job if you continue to behave as you do in class.

MARK: What do you mean?

T: Well, you've been late to class the past three mornings, and you always enter making a lot of noise, like you're seeking attention. I'm wondering how you think that might be viewed if it were on the job.

MARK: I would not be late on the job.

T: Oh, how would that be different?

MARK: I'd make myself get up earlier to be on time.

T: What about the job would make you want to get up earlier?

MARK: Well, I would not want to lose the job.

T: So, if you want something, like keeping the job, then you can get up on time. Is that right?

MARK: I guess so.

T: I'm wondering what that tells you about being late for this class.

MARK: Probably that I don't care enough to get here on time.

T: Exactly. What do you think I should do about that?

MARK: Well . . . I don't think you can do anything. It has to be me who does something.

T: I agree. What do you think you can do?

MARK: I like the class and I know it's important for my future. I'll just have to force myself.

T: OK, that sounds good, but how are you going to act when you show up?

MARK: I'll behave.

T: Good. It might help to mentally practice this good behavior, like being on time, before you actually start it.

MARK: How can I do that?

T: Here's how. Picture yourself tomorrow morning, walking into class on time. Now picture how you are behaving.

MARK: OK.

T: Can you picture yourself doing that?

MARK: Yes.

T: What are you doing?

MARK: I've walked in . . . put my books on my desk . . . getting my calculator out, getting set for class. . . .

T: Great. How is how you are acting in your mental picture different from how you have been entering the class?

MARK: I'm not talking to everyone. I'm more polite to you.

T: That's good. What can I expect to see tomorrow morning?

MARK: I'll be on time . . . and I'll be good.

T: Thanks, Mark.

Obviously, the teacher's success was quicker than what might be expected in a "real" situation. However, the technique of future pacing, when done in a constructive fashion by a caring teacher, can help students *see* their behavior in a different light and provide them a useful vehicle for change. Future pacing is an excellent way to help students understand their present behavior by offering them a contrast with desired future behavior.

PRESCRIBING ACTION

Action prescriptions are "a form of homework, a set of detailed directions for the client to carry out after the counseling session" (Lee, Pulvino, & Perrone, 1994, p. 213). They can be used in teaching as well as counseling. They can take different forms and be focused in a number of directions. We will describe how teachers can use goal-, solution-, and exception-based action prescriptions to resolve conflicts.

Goal-Based Action Prescriptions

As stated earlier in the chapter, well-stated goals abide by the following conditions:

1. Goals are under the person's control.
2. Effective goals specify what students will be doing when on track toward achieving their goals.
3. Effective goal statements specify conditions under which action can be observed.
4. Effective goal statements may specify actions, in percentages, degrees, or numbers, that will be acceptable during a specific time period.
5. Effective goals are stated in a positive form.
6. Effective goals are stated in the students' language.

When goals adhere to these conditions, they automatically become action prescriptions. For instance, the following goal statements also constitute action prescriptions:

- I will start my class project as soon as the bell has rung for class to begin.
- I will turn in my homework at the beginning of the class period.
- I will work silently until I am called on to respond.
- I will ask for help anytime I feel stuck on a problem in class.
- I will work in the computer lab a minimum of 3 days a week.

Teachers can use action prescriptions by reiterating and encouraging students to carry out goal statements. By using action prescriptions in this manner, teachers help students reduce ambiguity and confusion, provide a specific focus for their activity, and subsequently reduce conflict.

Solution-Based Action Prescriptions

Action prescriptions can be used to help others learn or practice solutions to their problems. Lankton and Lankton (1986) suggest that in using this approach, several principles be kept in mind:

1. Identifying the needed solution behavior
2. Identifying a context in which the behavior can be learned or reinforced
3. Using resources from the person's life as part of the action prescription
4. Approaching the final solution in a gradual manner
5. Using an action prescription that is practiced indirectly and yet under the person's control

The goal in using solution-based action prescriptions is to help the individual experience a positive solution to a problem. By using a solution-based action prescription in a natural setting, teachers can help students develop helpful positive ways of behaving. When this can be done, tension is reduced and conflict is reduced or dissipated.

In the following example, a teacher uses a solution-based action prescription to help a student develop positive helpful behaviors. The teacher is concerned about the direction that Jason will take in his life. She believes that he could become a respected leader in the school or move in the opposite direction and become a negative figure. She is aware of his leadership skills and uses them in developing and employing her action prescription.

TEACHER: Jason, I am aware that you have a lot of friends and that you get along well with everybody.

JASON: I like most people.

T: That's good. And they seem to like you, too.

JASON: I guess so.

T: Jason, I have a problem and I would like your help. It has to do with your ability to get along with people.

JASON: What is it?

T: Well, I have a new student in one of my classes. He just moved here from Chicago. He's a pleasant young man, but he doesn't know anybody. I was wondering if you could help me help him.

JASON: What can I do?

T: I was wondering if you could make friends with him and introduce him to some of your friends. He seems interested in some of the things you are involved in. For instance, he mentioned an interest in the student council and the yearbook committee. What do you think? Could you help me and him out?

JASON: Sure. That's no big deal. What's his name?

T: Great! I appreciate it. So will he. His name is Todd.

JASON: How will I meet him?

T: I'll ask him to come to my room tomorrow when you have class with me. I'll introduce you.

JASON: That sounds OK to me.

T: Thank you, Jason. I appreciate your willingness to go out of your way to help Todd.

JASON: Sure.

The teacher involved Jason in positive behaviors that she believed would move him toward continued positive behaviors. To do this, she used his leadership skills, ability to make friends, and a number of his interests. In addition, she suggested avenues for involvement and facilitated the interaction. To follow up on the action prescription, the teacher would check with Jason at a future date. This would provide her an opportunity to see how the introductions worked out and to reinforce behavior that was encouraged with the solution-based action prescription.

Exception-based action prescriptions

Teachers may choose to use exception-based action prescriptions to help others move toward positive exceptions and away from problematic areas. For instance, if a student is focused on not being able to get along with a partner in group project, the teacher might refocus attention on when the student has worked effectively with the partner in the past. To do this, the teacher might say something such as this:

- I'd be interested in knowing what you did in the past to work effectively.
- Tell me what you did to work together in the past.
- How would others have seen you differently when you were working effectively in the past?

By focusing on the exception, the teacher increases its significance. When this exception is then prescribed, the student's behavior can change substantially. Through use of exception-based action prescriptions, that which begins as unusual behavior can become expected behavior. Consider the following example using an exception-based action prescription:

TEACHER: You say that you can never get your homework done on time. Can you think of any time when you could?

ANNA: Well, when we were working on that class project.

T: What were you doing differently then?

ANNA: I was spending time in study hall on it.

T: Tell me how can you make that happen now?

ANNA: I guess I could spend time when I'm not in class on it.

T: Are you willing to try that?

ANNA: Yes.

T: That sounds good.

Here the teacher focused on the exception when the homework did get completed. Once this was stated, it became possible for the teacher to use it as a basis for prescribing the exceptional action.

In conclusion, goal-, solution-, and exception-based action prescriptions can be used to provide others a stimulus for practicing needed behaviors. Through their careful application, teachers can foster student goal achievement and facilitate solution of problems. Through the use of exception-based action prescriptions, teachers can help students appreciate and use their skills, skills that are available at those times when they effectively confront their concerns.

TIME ZERO

Decker (1978) has developed a personal problem-solving approach termed Time Zero that can be used in conflict situations. Time Zero is conceptualized as the present point in time. This is distinguished from the past, when an individual accepts personal feelings as normal, and the future, when an individual achieves what he or she wants. Time Zero is a time for renewal and moving forward rather than looking back. Time Zero is consistent with solution-oriented constructs presented earlier in this chapter. It primarily consists of eight core concepts, four common errors and four problem-solving steps, which are presented here. We have used Time Zero to develop specific ways that each could be used by teachers in a school setting.

Common Pattern of Errors

When people encounter conflict situations, they go through a typical pattern of errors. Specifically, when a conflict occurs, those involved have a high emotional response that leads them to one or more of the following reactions.

Faulty Statement of the Problem

This response usually entails some form of generalization and/or irrational thinking:

- Nobody likes me!
- Everyone is out to get me!
- Teachers think I'm stupid!
- I'm just dumb! That's why this happened!
- I'll never get this stuff. It's too hard!

These forms of generalizations and irrational thinking result from a person's high emotionality. Under normal circumstances, with low emotionality, the same person would not make these statements. However, in the heat of the conflict, there is a tendency to overreact.

Impulsive Explanation

Generally, in the impulsive explanation, responsibility for conflict is attributed to others. The impulsive explanation can take a variety of forms but usually includes blaming someone or something else for causing the conflict.

- Nobody likes me! If I could afford clothes like theirs, then they would like me.
- Everyone is out to get me! They think I'm a teacher's pet because I answer all his questions!
- Teachers think I'm stupid! If they gave fair tests, they would not think I'm stupid!
- I'm just dumb! My parents raised me wrong!
- I'll never get this stuff. It's too hard! Why don't they write books you can understand?

In each of these examples, the person blames someone or something for conflict being experienced. Blaming allows the person to avoid personal responsibility.

Impulsive Solution

Very often, when students' emotions are highly activated, they not only blame others for the situation but also come up with a solution that is self-defeating.

- Nobody likes me! I just won't go to school anymore!
- Everyone is out to get me! They think I'm a teacher's pet because I answer his questions! I'll show them. I won't say anything in class anymore!
- Teachers think I'm stupid! I can stop doing any homework because they think I'm stupid anyway!
- I'm just dumb! My parents raised me wrong! I'll never try that again!
- I'll never get this stuff. It's too hard! Why don't they write books you can understand? I just won't read it anymore!

In each of the examples, the student has suggested a self-defeating solution to the situation. The solution will make the original situation worse.

Plea for Endorsement

Very often when students experience conflict, they want others to approve of and agree with their definition of the problem. They do this by making either an explicit or implicit plea for endorsement. They want others to agree with their definition of the problem, their impulsive explanation, their impulsive solution, or some combination of the three.

- Nobody likes me! It's my clothes! I'll just not go to school anymore! You can understand why I have a problem, can't you? (plea for endorsement of the impulsive explanation)
- Everyone is out to get me! They think I'm a teacher's pet because I answer your questions! I'll show them. I won't say anything in class anymore! Isn't that what you would do? (plea for endorsement of the impulsive solutions)
- Teachers think I'm stupid! It's because of my test scores, that's why! I guess I can stop doing any homework because they think I'm stupid anyway! You can understand why I feel that way! (plea for endorsement of the faulty statement of the problem)
- I'm just dumb! That's why this happened! I guess my parents raised me wrong! I'll never try that again! I guess there is nothing I can do. (indirect plea for endorsement for faulty statement of the problem, the impulsive explanation, and the impulsive solution)
- I'll never get this stuff. It's too hard! Why don't they write books you can understand? I just won't read it anymore! I'm sure you have felt the same way! (plea for endorsement of the impulsive explanation)

It is important to be aware of these potential patterns of errors that students manufacture when they become highly emotional in conflict situations. Such awareness and recognition will help prevent you from getting caught up in side issues that might increase or maintain conflict.

Moving to Problem Solving

If caught in a conflict, center yourself and use a confluent response by acknowledging the other person's feelings. If you are mediating between two others, use a confluent response to recognize each person's right to have their feelings. This focuses on the present, the here and now of experience: a place to begin moving toward restoration of harmony.

- Nobody likes me! I look in the mirror and then I know why. It's my clothes! I just won't go to school anymore! You can understand why I have a problem, can't you?

T: You're feeling different and unliked.

- Everyone is out to get me! They think I'm a teacher's pet because I answer questions! I'll show them. I won't say anything in class anymore! Isn't that what you would do?

T: You're feeling picked on and you don't have any choice.

- Teachers think I'm stupid! It's because of my test scores, that's why! I guess I can stop doing any homework because they think I'm stupid anyway! You can understand why I feel that way!

T: You sound very discouraged and ready to give up.

- I'm just dumb! That's why this happened! I guess my parents raised me wrong! I'll never try that again! I guess there is nothing I can do.

T: You sound like you're feeling that things are hopeless.

- I'll never get this stuff. It's too hard! Why don't they write books you can understand? I just won't read it anymore! I'm sure you have felt the same way!

T: You sound very frustrated.

It may take more than one response to calm a person. Continue making confluent responses, maintaining a common theme, until the person has a more relaxed state of mind. Then apply the following four steps.

Identify the Trigger Event

Because students go through the pattern of errors described earlier, they tend to overgeneralize and lose their focus. One way to help them regain focus is to identify the event that triggered their present emotional state. The trigger event is one specific stimulus that provided impetus for the individual's current emotional state. Explorations similar to the following can be used to identify trigger events:

- What specifically happened that you got so . . . (fill in the blank with the identified emotion)?
- What one thing seemed to start all of this?
- Describe for me specifically who did what that started all of this.
- Tell me what triggered all of this.
- I want to know what one thing got all of this started.

You may need to repeatedly probe with confluent responses before the student can identify the trigger event. Once the trigger event is identified, you can move on to the next step of problem solving.

Help the Person Decide What Is Next

Often, at the center of conflict are thwarted needs, desires, or goals. The way to keep focus on problem solving is to help the student decide what she or he would like to have happen next. Care must be taken in this step to shape responses so that they are under the person's control. That is, goals that require others to change, the system to change, or the environment to be different do not move toward restoration of harmony. Although it may be true that others may need to change, the system needs to be changed, or the environment could be improved, those are goals to be dealt with after the immediate conflict is managed. Explorations similar to the following can be used:

- What do you want to have happen?
- What will have to happen for you to be satisfied?
- What needs to happen for you to get on track to getting what you want?
- Tell me what you want to happen now.
- I'd like to know what you would like to happen next.

It is acceptable for students to state that they want changes in others, the system, or environment as long as their next step focuses on their personal actions to bring about desired outcomes. For example:

TEACHER: What do you want to have happen?

SAM: I'd like Mr. Hershey to get off my back!

This may be an acceptable statement as long as the next step focuses on how the student's own actions will make this happen.

Help the Person Develop a Plan

Once you have helped the student decide what should happen next, it is time to develop a plan of action to accomplish the goal. The plan can be as simple as avoiding the other person(s) involved in the conflict or avoiding the conflict situation. Or the plan can be an elaborate strategy. Explorations similar to the following can be used to help people develop a plan of action:

- What do you have to do to make what you want happen?
- Tell me what you're going to do to accomplish that.
- What can you do to make that happen?
- I'd like to know what you're going to do to make that happen.

Notice that each of these explorations focus responsibility on the student by asking what actions he or she is going to take. Returning to our previous example:

TEACHER: What do you want to have happen?

SAM: I'd like Mr. Hershey to get off my back!

T: What are you going to do to get Mr. Hershey off your back?

SAM: Well, I guess I could do my homework.

T: What else do you do that Mr. Hershey gets on your back for?

SAM: I guess he gets on me the most when I fool around in class.

T: Well, what can you do about this to get him off your back?

SAM: I guess I could keep my mouth shut and not fool around.

T: How are you going to do that?

SAM: When I feel myself about to talk or fool around, I'll write myself a note.

T: What will it say?

SAM: Something like, "Knock it off now!"

The teacher, in this example, keeps the focus on actions the student is going to take rather than on how Mr. Hershey is going to change. Focus on the student's actions is necessary to get past the pattern of errors.

Help the Person Decide Specific Steps to Take

Even though a plan has been established, it is necessary to develop a specific set of steps to implement the plan. This can be accomplished by answering a series of simple questions:

- **Who** is going to do . . . ?
- **What** will these people do?
- **Where** will they do it?
- **When** will they do it?
- **How** will you recognize that it has been accomplished?

Answering these questions specifies steps to be taken and timing that should occur. Such specific steps provide a basis for future follow-up to examine the action plan's effectiveness.

Summary of Time Zero

It is important to recognize the common pattern of errors people make when involved in a conflict situation. They include

- faulty statement of the problem,
- impulsive explanation,
- some form of an impulsive solution, and
- a plea for endorsement.

By using confluent responses, teachers can recognize individuals' right to have feelings, calm them down, and move to the here and now as a basis for moving toward a restoration of harmony. After returning to the here and now, teachers can move toward problem solving by doing the following:

- Identifying the trigger event
- Helping the person decide what next
- Helping the person develop a plan
- Helping the person decide the steps to take

EXAMPLES: APPLICATION OF TIME ZERO TO SCHOOL-BASED CONFLICT MANAGEMENT

Example 1: A principal reacts to a teacher for the way she perceives the teachers' students are acting. Please note the principal's opening statement. It demonstrates a faulty statement of the problem, an impulsive explanation with the teacher as the "bad guy," an impulsive solution, and a plea for endorsement.

P: You have to get your kids to be quiet. You can hear them all over the school. You are not in control of your class. You have the noisiest class in this building. If you can't get them to behave, then I will. Don't you understand the position this puts me in?

T: You caught me by surprise. I did not realize you felt my students were out of control.

P: Well, they are and you better do something about it.

T: I would have thought Mr. Allis next door would have said something to me about this. I'm sorry it seems like my students are out of control. They seem to be learning OK, but I don't want them to be disturbing others.

P: Hmm!

T: Could you help me? What specifically did my students do that got your attention?

P: As soon as I came up the stairs, I could hear kids from your room.

T: I see. So, it's today you are talking about? More specifically, within the last few minutes.

P: That's right.

T: OK, that helps. I think I know what the problem is and how it can be remedied. Thanks for the input.

P: You're welcome.

In this example, the teacher gets the principal to identify the trigger event and suggests that the principal's input will be used to arrive at a satisfactory solution to the problem. Note that the teacher maintains a confluent perspective throughout the interchange with the principal. This approach maximizes the possibility that harmony will be restored.

Example 2: Consider the following middle school situation in which a teacher finds herself mediating a conflict between two students who belong to two competing cliques. Her intervention is complex because combatants are "playing" to separate audiences and are unresponsive to her direct overtures.

GAIL: If you had a brain in your head, you would not act so dumb.

CHRIS: You and your friends would not have a brain if you put your heads together. How can you call me dumb? You've got to be halfway intelligent to know whether I have a brain and you're not even a half-wit.

TEACHER: Whoa! You two are about to erupt. I want to know what set each of you off. Gail, tell me what upset you first, then Chris, tell me what upset you. I want you both to close your eyes while I listen to what each of you have to say.

GAIL/CHRIS: Why do we have to close our eyes?

TEACHER: It will be easier for me to hear what each of you have to say if I can focus on your words rather than how you treat each other. OK, Gail, what did Chris say or do to upset you and when did she do it? . . . OK, Chris, what did Gail say or do to upset you and when did he do it? . . . I can see that you both are upset and both of you believe that you have a legitimate reason for feeling the way you do. So, what do we do about your conflict? Since you can't shout one another down and we don't allow fighting in school, what do you want to have happen?

CHRIS: I'd feel a lot better if I could tell Gail off and never see or hear him again.

GAIL: Me too.

TEACHER: Are one of you going to transfer to another school tomorrow? Because you both are shaking your heads no, I guess that won't be happening. Since you are going to see and hear each other and I won't let you yell or fight, what else can you do?

At this point, the teacher has identified the trigger event, calmed the situation, established boundaries for interaction (i.e., no shouting and no fighting), and has started working toward solution generation. The plan that results may be no more than a truce in which students agree to avoid each other or "turn the other cheek" rather than "attack" at the mere sight of one another. The teacher probably would not attempt to have the students become friends. Rather, she would attempt to resolve the open conflict and have the students behave in an acceptable manner.

Both of these illustrative situations would take no more than a few minutes. Both stop the flow of interaction, focus on the here and now, and move toward harmony—not necessarily toward embracing one another or achieving common ground.

SUMMARY

This chapter presents five solution-oriented constructs and one problem-solving model for reaching present-time conflict management. Social responsibility was examined from the perspective of contracts, how behavior leads to consequences, and how commitments can lead to action. The three issues of finding exceptions, goal setting, and future pacing were then presented. Three ways of prescribing action were described: goal-based action prescriptions, solution-focused action prescriptions, and exception-based action prescriptions. Finally, the problem-solving model of Time Zero was discussed in detail.

REFERENCES

Decker, J. P. (1978). *Solving personality clashes with time zero*. Tempe, AZ: Synecology.

Lankton, S. R., & Lankton, C. J. (1986). *Enchantment and intervention in family therapy*. New York: Brunner/Mazel.

Lee, J. L., Pulvino, C. J., & Perrone, P. A. (1994). *Dynamic counseling*. Minneapolis, MN: Educational Media.

Luft, J. (1969). *Of human interaction: The Johari model*. Palo Alto, CA: Mayfield.

Maslow, A. (1969). *Motivation and personality*. New York: Harper & Row.

ADDITIONAL RESOURCES

Cade, B. (1993). *A brief guide to brief therapy*. New York: Norton.

deShazer, S. (1994). *Words were originally magic*. New York: Norton.

Gilligan, S. G., & Price, R. (Eds.). (1993). *Therapeutic conversations*. New York: Norton.

Lankton, S. (1980). *Practical magic*. Cupertino, CA: Meta.

O'Hanlon, W. H., & Davis-Weiner, M. (1989). *In search of solutions*. New York: Norton.

CHAPTER 8

Managing Schools and Classrooms to Minimize Disruptive Behavior

The interventions that we describe in this chapter are presented to minimize the potential for conflict. They also can be used by teachers to create an educational atmosphere that is conducive to learning.

The chapter has been divided into two major sections. In the first section we examine the work of a number of authors from whom we abstract principles useful for teachers in managing conflict. In the second section we take an in-depth look at four ways of managing student behavior. The four strategies that we examine are built on concepts of permitting, tolerating, preventing, and interrupting.

PRINCIPLES

Principle 1: Use Reason to Reduce the Degree of Negative Emotion

Saaty and Alexander (1989) note that when a conflict arises, it is necessary to find an outcome that, at a minimum, represents improvement in the present situation for one of the parties and a worsening of the situation for no one. This can be accomplished when involved parties are helped to overcome initial emotional responses. The teacher's use of reason or logic may be the best way to establish a facilitative, conflict-free classroom atmosphere. Reason or logic can be used to overcome the typical emotional characteristic of most conflict situations. By relying on reason, teachers can defuse negative situations and prepare students for positive change.

The general guide, suggested by Saaty and Alexander, for creating a classroom environment in which debilitating conflicts will be at a minimum requires that teachers maintain a reason-emotion ratio favoring reason. Teachers must be able to recognize emotionally charged situations, be aware of rational problem-solving strategies, and be prepared to apply specific intervention strategies that reduce "heat" while enhancing "light."

The following example demonstrates how this might be done. Bill, the student, is so upset that his face has turned red and his eyes are bugging out. He has been working for 2 weeks on a science-engineering project, a bridge made out of cardboard that will support over 100 pounds. One of his classmates, Fred, jumped on the bridge, and it came tumbling down.

> TEACHER: Alright. Everyone step back. Bill, we need to assess the damage and see what we can do to help you rebuild the bridge.
>
> BILL: He did it on purpose—he couldn't wait to break it. I'm going to break his head!
>
> FRED: Bull—if you were so great, it wouldn't break.
>
> T: Bill, I think we can make this right, but you have to tell me what materials you need, and we have to figure out when you can work on the bridge. Fred is going to be your assistant.
>
> BILL: I don't want his help—he doesn't know how to help anybody do anything.

FRED: You can't make me help him.

T: Bill, start making a list of what you need. Fred, make a list of the stores that might receive packages in thin cardboard boxes. I will pick up enough boxes tonight so we can start tomorrow. We also need a safer place to reassemble the bridge. Bill and Fred, I want you to come up with two or three good ways to protect the bridge while it is being rebuilt. Before I start the next lesson, I'll be back and you can tell me what you think, and I'll pick the idea that seems best. Now get your heads together and come up with a plan so this won't happen again.

In this situation, the teacher would have to keep her eye on the two boys and perhaps remind them that they have to come up with a plan before moving on. The key task is to reduce emotion by helping the boys think positively while doing something constructive. Because their energy is going to exist, it is better to channel it quickly and constructively—the aikido principle of blending and redirecting. An effective approach is to get them to substitute planning for reacting. This will decelerate conflict. The teacher may have to remain on the scene as a physical barrier until emotions can cool and positive action begins. Note that apologies from Fred can come later—and should.

Principle 2: Judicious Use of Rules Is Important in Conflict Management

Froyen (1984) expands the conceptualization of teachers as managers of the classroom to include more specifically their being managers of students' behavior. He suggests that teachers can minimize classroom conflicts by using a minimum number of "rules for behavior." Froyen states that rules should be meaningful to students, enforceable by teachers, and used to assure that students feel physically and psychologically secure. Rules should be openly discussed. Students should be provided guidelines for their actions and be informed regarding the consequences of their behavior. By focusing on rules and on guidelines for how they will be carried out, teachers can minimize negative feelings and consequent emotional outbursts while maximizing positive feelings and rational decision making. This process provides students and teachers concrete behavior to be aware of and a strategy for dealing with behavior that breaks the rules. It typically results in more open communication and reduces conflict. Examine the following interchange to see how this can be accomplished:

TEACHER: Class, there are just two rules for how we behave in my class. We do not go into another person's space, and we do not interrupt others. First, I want everyone to take one of these long pieces of string and mark your space around your seats. Now everyone look where everyone has placed their strings. Do any of you think someone has too much space? Do any of you think you have too little space? Let's move the strings until everyone is satisfied. What are ways we can ask if we can come into someone's space? If they say no, how do we act? If someone says no and you go into their space uninvited, what should be done? Class, I'll write your ideas on the board and we will decide on which two or three we can all live with.

Now, let's do the same about talking and listening. This will be harder because we don't have any string to set boundaries. Since words can penetrate any barrier, we need some listening and talking rules that we can practice until we can do it without thinking. First, is there anytime it is OK to interrupt? When someone hogs all the words, how can we interrupt?

STUDENTS: *[They provide a number of responses to these questions.]*

T: OK, whoa—those are good suggestions. I'll write them on the board. Should we allow people to make an "honest" mistake?

SUE: Sure.

T: OK, once in awhile someone will forget and if I think it's a mistake, I'll just hold up my hand and motion for them to wait. How about if someone keeps breaking the rule?

SAM: We think that's different. They should be made to follow the rule.

T: All right, that person will have to repeat what the person they interrupted has said until everyone agrees that they are paying attention.

Principle 3: Appropriate Discipline Can Lessen Conflict

Charles (1992) views rules from a slightly different perspective. He recommends that teachers establish classroom rules that fit the hierarchy of student misbehavior. For Charles, the punishment should fit the crime and be presented in the most timely way. He identifies the following five levels of student behaviors that call for teacher responses:

1. *Goofing off*—failing to attend or continuously getting off task
2. *Disrupting the class*—engaging in behavior that interferes with normal class activity
3. *Defying authority*—failing to obey or inappropriately challenging authority
4. *Immorality*—engaging in acts of cheating, lying, stealing, or similar activities
5. *Overt aggression*—participating in physical and/or verbal attacks

The first two sets of behaviors can escalate into conflict in the classroom. Failing to obey might be classroom specific or a response to school rules, in which case the response differs. Defying system authority and the two more serious offenses require decisive, thoughtful, controlled responses. All are best handled if there are school rules and procedures that are known and enforced. If teachers can effectively manage the first two levels, the likelihood of the third level, defiance of authority, can be lessened.

Charles (1992) suggests that the most effective way to diminish these behaviors is to help offending students "save face" with peers while insisting that students adhere to classroom and school rules. Teachers can do so by avoiding embarrassing or belittling students in front of their peers regardless of the act. To do this, they may have to use a nonspecific response when the transgression occurs and postpone specific feedback to the student until later in the day. This approach overcomes the need for students to fight back and/or to defy authority or to escalate the conflict situation. By handling transgressions privately, teachers can help students maintain self-respect and peer respect while providing themselves time to consider the best possible long-term course of action. **It is important to let the offending student know immediately that the behavior must stop**. The following interchange in which a student is disrupting the class illustrates how this principle can be applied.

Mary is making faces, squirming in her seat, making funny noises, and doing just about anything to capture the class' attention. The most effective teacher response is to position herself close to Mary without changing her tone of voice or without disrupting the flow of the class. After a few moments, when the class's attention is no longer focused on Mary, the teacher can quietly tell Mary that she wants to talk with her after class. As the teacher moves away, she should maintain eye contact without staring. As soon as an opportunity arises to talk with Mary, beyond the eyes and ears of her classmates, the teacher should tell her that she does not accept her behavior and that if it persists, she will call Mary's parent(s) to discuss the behavior. The teacher can then ask Mary for an explanation of her behavior. In conclusion, it is important for teachers to maintain firm control while modeling behavior that they want their students to demonstrate.

Principle 4: Preparing Students for Every Circumstance Can Lessen Conflict

Kameenui and Darch (1995) suggest that at the beginning of the year, students should be taught how to behave in every circumstance for which teachers expect appropriate behavior. They believe that this approach provides students a rehearsal for the school year and their part in it. In Kameenui and Darch's plan, teachers write the script, direct the student-actors, and offer students extra coaching when needed. The teacher applauds successful performances and helps struggling students learn and practice until they perform satisfactorily. This is a proactive approach that expends energy to bolster positive performances rather than a reactionary perspective in which energy is spent overcoming negative transgressions.

Kameenui and Darch believe that teachers can help students become better school citizens by helping them understand how positive behaviors rehearsed in the classroom can be used throughout the school building. Through in-class rehearsal, students can be helped to make the transition to outside activities in the cafeteria and gym, on the playground, in other classrooms, and even coming and going from home to school. Teachers can use this in-class rehearsal to sensitize students to many important aspects of their total education. For instance, in rehearsals, teachers can expand students' awareness of gender and culture differences, differences in students' information-processing or learning styles, modes of communication, what is upsetting to individuals, and how each student's behavior affects others.

Rehearsal can be useful in a wide variety of ways. For instance, consider the mathematics teacher who believes that it is important for students to learn group-interactive problem-solving skills. This teacher knows that students have not been prepared for this type of activity. He decides that to prepare students for what will be a regular class activity, one that is central to development of problem-solving skills, he will have to prepare students for this activity before it is needed. To do this, the teacher can discuss the purpose of group problem solving, demonstrate a group problem-solving activity, and involve students in an activity that will prepare them for the group process that will be used in future classes.

Principle 5: Teach Students How to Give and Receive Feedback

Feedback is an essential ingredient in the educational process. At times this essential process is viewed as being harmful or negative. Teachers can overcome this tendency by preparing students to understand the purpose of feedback and the useful role that it plays in learning. They can accomplish this by helping students consider the following guidelines for giving and receiving feedback:

1. When giving feedback, consider how you would like someone to provide you feedback. In offering feedback, be aware of how you feel and what you think. Take your time in providing feedback. If you do not communicate your thoughts effectively at first, correct yourself and start again.

2. When receiving feedback, listen to what is being said. Be aware of how you feel and what you think. Take a deep breath, try to smile, repeat what you said, and ask for clarification if needed.

3. Judge the feedback. If further information is needed, ask for it specifically.

By teaching students how to give and receive feedback, teachers can help students minimize emotion and maximize reason. We are not suggesting that the objective is to eliminate emotion from the learning experience. In fact, if learning is devoid of emotion, learning probably will be diminished. As a rule of thumb, however, the ratio of reason to emotion should favor reason. Once students learn to use this process, they can apply it in many interactions and, subsequently, be less dependent on teachers to act in mediating roles. Consider the following exchange:

TEACHER: Let's have Bill share with Mary what he thinks of her poem.

BILL: Mary, it would be hard for me to write a poem and then read it to the class. I don't know much about poetry, but shouldn't the words rhyme?

MARY: Bill, there are many forms of poetry. Did you feel at all sad when you heard my poem? I was trying to express how a young person feels when no one seems to like them.

BILL: I guess I didn't listen to your poem that way. I was expecting the last words to rhyme, and when they didn't I got confused. Would you read it again and I'll try to listen differently?

MARY: (Reads poem slowly and with more effect)

BILL: I don't know what I feel. Why doesn't she just make friends and then she won't be alone and feeling sorry for herself?

MARY: Maybe I have to set the stage more so you will understand how she got to where she is. I was concentrating on how she felt, but I can see why you would be confused. Thanks, that helps.

BILL: What did I do? All I said was I didn't understand why she didn't do something instead of just feeling bad.

MARY: If my poem confuses you, then I need to work on it so you understand the situation and can identify a little with her feelings. That's what is helpful.

If students can treat one another with respect and replace judgmental statements with honest questions, then they are providing one another the most constructive form of feedback. For this dialogue to work, students need to trust one another and feel a sense of belonging and community in the classroom. Interestingly, certain rules of behavior, when maintained, help create this kind of classroom environment.

In summary, five principles have been presented that teachers can use to manage conflict: (a) use reason to reduce the degree of negative emotion, (b) judicious use of rules is important in conflict management, (c) appropriate discipline can lessen conflict, (d) preparing students for every circumstance can lessen conflict, and (e) teaching students how to give and receive feedback can facilitate student control and behavior.

STUDENT BEHAVIOR: MANAGEMENT STRATEGIES

We believe that the use of the principles just presented can help teachers manage conflict in the classroom. Teachers will be most effective when they couple use of the principles with their knowledge of students and student behaviors. The writings of Long and Newman (1961) can facilitate this coupling.

Long and Newman describe four major categories for handling student behavior. The four strategies are built on concepts of permitting, tolerating, preventing, and interrupting. Teachers must use each, in the right combination and at the right time, for each student in each situation.

Permitting Strategies

When teachers set limits through class rules and establish overt sanctioning behaviors, students will have less need to test limits. By setting positive expectations and negative consequences, teachers can create an educational atmosphere that limits the potential for conflict. Grade school children can be told that it is OK to run, shout, and scream on the playground; to be physically free when working with art materials; and/or to use the lavatory at specific times. High school students can be allowed to talk in the cafeteria, choose when to use library facilities, or make decisions about who they team up with on class projects. Classes may have ground rules for asking questions and expressing opposing views. Knowledge of school and classroom rules helps students feel reassured. If students know in advance that teachers, administrators, or fellow students will not disapprove of their behavior, they will be less likely to act inappropriately. Some examples of permitting behavior include these:

- During independent work, you may sharpen your pencil, get a drink, get a piece of scratch paper from the back of the room, or get a pass to the bathroom.
- After you have completed your assignment, you may go to the learning center, get a book from the class library, or work on your science assignment.
- On the playground you may run, shout, jump, and climb.

Tolerating Strategies

Sometimes classroom behavior that is contrary to the rules may be tolerated. However, toleration should not be confused with approving the behavior. Realistically, students probably will make mistakes since very few can follow perfectly all contracts "made" in school. In general, three sources of behavior can sometimes be tolerated: learner excitement or frustration; behaviors that reflect transitions in social, emotional, or conceptual development; and behavior symptomatic of disease.

Learner Excitement or Frustration

Whenever students learn new concepts and experiment with new ideas, the potential arises for increased excitement or frustration. Both can lead to behavior normally considered to be "outside" the rules. Also, frustration can be exacerbated by certain myths regarding success and failure that provide a basis for feeling guilty or inadequate. (Chapter 12 provides an overview of these myths.)

Behavior That Reflects Transitions in Development Stages

Some behavior is age typical and will change as students mature. Change can occur within a few days at particularly volatile periods of development. Attempts to alter, inhibit, or control typical behaviors usually result in such negligible changes that they are not worth inevitable confrontations. Tolerance and understanding, without sanction or approval, will prevent needless confrontations if the teacher can be patient during the developmental process. For example, most students in the early grades are impulsive and motor oriented. Learning typically is kinesthetic. Kindergarten teachers accept this and learn to accommodate or tolerate such behavior. They do not allow wild or severe acting-out behaviors, but they do not create unnecessary confrontations by attempting to control what is largely uncontrollable. Another example, common among third- and fourth-grade students, is loyalty to the teacher, manifested in many ways. One such way is through the process of tattling on others: "Mr. Samuel, John pulled Mary's hair!" "Mrs. Panzer, when you were out in the hall, Jimmy pulled a leaf off the plant on your desk!" "Miss Pratt, do you know that Jill copied her homework from Jack?" Other examples of developmentally typical behavior are the disheveled appearance of many preadolescent boys, the primping of many eighth- and ninth-grade girls, the dress fads of male and female students in high school, and the uniforms of gang members. Such behaviors are not to be condoned, approved, or sanctioned but under most circumstances can be tolerated by teachers as part of normal developmental stage behavior.

A classroom example might further illustrate what we mean by tolerating age- or developmentally related behavior. One of the most difficult situations that teachers have to deal with is the mating ritual of middle school boys and girls. Typically, boys show attention to targeted girls by roughhousing or by being physically abusive. Girls may welcome the attention but not the form that it takes. Boys usually lack the social skills to pay special attention to a girl in a way that is acceptable to both the boy's peers and to the targeted young woman. When the roles are reversed and girls are paying attention to a targeted boy, the girl's social skills may be more appropriate, but the boy may not know how to respond appropriately. Essentially boys and girls are not comfortable in forming relationships in early adolescence. By organizing small-group learning activities in which girls and boys are provided guidelines for cooperative work, teachers can assist the socialization process within the learning process.

Behavior Symptomatic of Disease

Behavior discussed so far might occur within any typical student. However, for a relatively few students, inappropriate behavior may occur because of illness. Usually such students are identified early in their school careers and provided specific assistance. Specialists such as school counselors, psychologists, social workers, special education teachers, and/or speech therapists are frequently enlisted to help such students moderate and control inappropriate behavior. However, some students may miss early detection. In those cases when physical or abnormal psychological behavior has not been previously detected, teachers are advised to refer the student to the most appropriate school resource. This referral resource typically is the school counselor or principal.

Preventing Strategies

Sometimes disruptive, potentially conflict-producing behaviors can be avoided by designing more developmentally appropriate school and classroom procedures. Sometimes school rules not only fail to prevent conflicts but may invite conflicts. Teachers who establish long lists of strict rules and attempt enforcing them will contribute to increasing the likelihood of conflict with their own students. According to Valentine (1987), a teacher's communication pattern also may contribute to conflicts with students.

Valentine draws attention to several ineffective communication patterns that teachers might want to avoid. Three of these patterns are difficult to change (i.e., ignoring inappropriate behavior, using negative body language, and being incongruent in verbal–nonverbal communication). Recently, it has been suggested that teachers should ignore student behaviors when they determine that the student is seeking attention. However, by ignoring behavior, the student, and other students, may believe that the teacher is condoning the behavior. Also, the offending student may behave increasingly obtusely until the teacher responds.

A number of strategies for responding are outlined in this book. In general, however, we suggest that a confluent response is the most appropriate. A positive teacher response is one in which the behavior is confronted in a way that its inappropriateness is noted and the student is allowed to save face.

Valentine's second observation centers on body language. Avoiding negative body language and having one's verbal and nonverbal behavior be congruent all the time are difficult to enact. One way to achieve positive and consistent body language is to solicit a colleague's help. Ask your colleague to observe you in your interactions with students. Use the specific feedback to understand and, where appropriate, amend your behavior.

Other problematic communication patterns include these:

- Encouraging inappropriate behavior ("I dare you!")
- Focusing on irrelevant behaviors
- Providing abstract or incomplete instructions
- Labeling students according to their behavior ("You are a ____!")
- Making negative predictions ("Some day you are going to end up a ____!")
- Asking "why?"—and not liking or accepting the answer
- Threatening punishment ("If you keep that up, I will ____!")
- Handing out a punishment that does not fit the offense (either too much or too little)

Because conflicts involve institutional rules as well as personalities, when teachers and administrators observe repeated conflicts occurring around similar issues and involving certain students, questions such as the following should be considered:

What are we doing to contribute to these conflicts?

Are any of these behaviors we observe developmentally typical?

Do we need to better instruct our students regarding how to behave?

In asking such questions, educators may discover that the solutions for problems lie in putting a different frame around the behaviors in question. Two examples of how school personnel reframed conflictual behaviors to solve particular problems follow.

In a large elementary school in the heart of Detroit, the staff's major problem during winter months was snowballing. Although additional teachers were scheduled for playground duty and the severity of the penalty was increased, the problem did not diminish. Students still threw snowballs, but they were much more clever about it. One teacher, tired of the additional playground duty, suggested that they paint a huge circular target on the back wall of the two-story school and actually program snowball throwing with a scoring system. After much discussion and apprehension, the idea was presented to students. They thought that it was a great idea. Consequently, a faculty-student committee was appointed to establish rules. Once the target was drawn, the problem of uncontrolled snowballing was virtually eliminated. Students threw all their energy into hitting the bull's-eye rather than one another. Some children would actually come to school early just so they could have the highest daily score. One teacher commented that many of the problem students were very active in this activity and threw themselves out by the time school started. He reported that they were even easier to teach.

A second example comes from a counselor in a midwestern high school. One fall, unidentified students began to write graffiti on lavatory walls and desks. Although teachers increased their surveillance and talked to their homeroom classes about defacing public property, graffiti writing continued and in fact increased. At a faculty meeting, the counselor suggested that the school set up a special graffiti wall outside of his office where there were normal bulletin boards. After some discussion of potential dangers (e.g., profanities), the staff decided to try the idea. The counselor met with the student council and presented the plan, and students eagerly endorsed it. A committee made up of students, a teacher, and the counselor met several times to discuss rules for using the graffiti wall. Two 4 × 8 foot panels of plywood were purchased and mounted on the wall outside the guidance office. The panels were painted white. A copy of graffiti-writing rules were posted on each of the panels. Several pencils and markers were mounted on the panels using strings and eye hooks. Rules for the graffiti board were announced in each homeroom. Policing of the graffiti wall was turned over to the student council. The graffiti wall became a popular diversion for students to express themselves creatively. When the graffiti wall was filled, it was repainted white so that it could be used again. The end result of this project was that graffiti writing in lavatories and on desks stopped completely.

These examples used an understanding of what caused the conflict and the principles of blending and redirecting from aikido. This understanding was used to reframe the behavior and solve the problem.

Interrupting Strategies

Teachers must regularly deal with spontaneous behavior in the classroom. Some student behavior needs to be controlled or inhibited to avoid conflicts and maintain an effective learning environment. Teachers need ways of interrupting disruptive behavior without escalating the problem. Teachers may wonder which behaviors to attend to and how they can efficiently and effectively interrupt potentially disruptive behavior before it becomes disruptive. This question cannot be answered without taking several things into consideration. However, Long and Newman (1961) provide criteria for judging when to interrupt potentially disruptive behavior. A brief review of each follows.

Reality Dangers

Teachers are more reality oriented than students, especially younger students, and are experienced in predicting consequences of student actions. When students are playing crazy games, fighting, or playing with something dangerous, teachers must use their experience and awareness as a basis for interceding.

Psychological Protection

Teachers can protect students from potential psychological injury as well as from potential physical injury. When students pick on a student, make derogatory remarks, or use racial nicknames, then teacher intervention is warranted. Interrupting negative behavior not only provides psychological protection for students but also helps prevent future conflicts.

Protection of School Property

When teachers observe situations in which school property can be damaged, action is called for. However, teachers must act in ways that do not suggest that the property is more important than students. To ignore the destruction of school property will be interpreted by students as meaning that teachers do not care and may lead them to think, "Why should I care?"

Protection against Negative Contagion

When teachers become aware that students with great social influence are beginning to engage in disruptive behavior and that tension and potential conflict are mounting, teachers need to interrupt the behavior before it spreads to other students in the classroom.

Highlighting the Importance of a School Policy

A teacher may interrupt not because students are misbehaving but to illustrate the value of a school rule or school policy. For example, a teacher might want to demonstrate why it is impossible for everyone to be first in line or how poor communication, or distortion of information, can lead to misunderstanding and conflict.

Avoiding Conflicts outside the Classroom

Teachers are justified in expecting students to adhere to certain behavioral rules when they are attending school assemblies, visiting community agencies, or participating in field trips. When controls built into classroom management are removed, special attention must be given to providing students other forms for controlling their behavior.

Depending on the developmental level of students, varying degrees of chaos should be expected in classrooms and schools. As mentioned, some age- or developmentally related behavior can be expected and tolerated. Teachers will experience less stress if they become comfortable with such behaviors. All these points of intervention are guides for determining when or what to interrupt. We realize that it will be impossible for a teacher to think through all of these possibilities before deciding whether to act and how to act. However, the guidelines described here can serve as reference points for teachers when considering whether to interrupt students.

A number of different strategies for interrupting behavior will be discussed next. They are used to prevent conflict from erupting if a well-designed set of classroom and school rules are in place. These strategies are not presented in any prioritized way; rather, they are independent strategies that may be applied in various situations using guidelines presented earlier. Most of the strategies are maximally effective at the beginning of the potentially disruptive behavior (i.e., nipping it in the bud).

Planned Ignoring

Simply calling attention to certain behaviors can reinforce the behavior. Assuming that the behavior will not become contagious, it is sometimes better to ignore it and avoid providing the student any gratification from the attention of the class and the teacher. For example, a student may be "reading" his book upside down and holding it out for everyone to see. You can tell him to hold the book upright—thereby drawing attention to him—or you can ignore him to the point when he becomes self-conscious and, if also ignored by the class, ends this attempt at gaining attention. However, stopping the behavior does not mean that what motivated the behavior does not still lurk in the student's mind or that the student will not try something else. When self-consciousness kicks in, you have accessed a natural, internal process that is working on your behalf—namely, no one wants to look foolish even if they are playing the fool.

How does the teacher know whether to ignore the behavior and whether the behavior is spontaneous or typical behavior for this student? At the beginning of the school year, a teacher may have difficulty differentiating between spontaneous behavior and behavior symptomatic of something disturbing the student. The work of Dreikurs, Grunwold, and Pepper (1982) can be helpful in this decision. They suggest that students are motivated to act out by needs such as gaining attention, overcoming feelings of inadequacy, seeking additional power, or taking revenge. By using these possibilities as hypotheses for the student's behavior, teachers can gain a better understanding of students in specific situations and use them to generate specific courses of action. For example, if the teacher determines that the student is feeling inadequate, he would probably respond quite differently than if he had decided that the student was seeking power.

Teachers also can monitor changes in individuals' behavior and emotions to protect students who are feeling stressed. Sadness, guilt, depression, anxiety, anger, tension, fear, and fatigue are emotions that teachers may want to attend to. Students exhibiting these emotions may need someone to hear their story and provide them with coping strategies. At times, teachers can do this. At other times, teachers may want to refer students to other school professionals such as school counselors or psychologists. No matter which strategy is used, however, if students remain members of the class, teachers may need to employ instructional strategies to protect individual students without isolating them.

Immediate Interruption

Successful teachers develop a variety of nonverbal signals to communicate approval and disapproval. Usually, these nonverbal techniques can be used to interrupt potential disruptive behavior before it explodes. These nonverbal techniques include such things as direct eye contact, hand gestures to sit down or be quiet, tapping or snapping of fingers, clearing of the throat, facial frowns, or pointing.

Proximity Control

Teachers know how effective it is to move closer to a student who is exhibiting potentially disruptive behavior. Standing near a student's desk can provide support for a student having difficulty learning the material. Standing near a student who is acting in a disruptive manner provides control while minimally embarrassing the student.

Boosting Interest

If student interest is waning and she or he is showing signs of restlessness or becoming frustrated with what is happening in class, it may be helpful for the teacher to show interest in the student and her or his work. Asking about the student's work or mentioning something of particular interest to that student can help the student refocus and mobilize energies on the task at hand. Additional interest may activate a student's natural motivation to please the teacher.

Inevitably, all students' attention will wander. We are concerned here with those students whose attention has left and not returned. If the pace of instruction is contributing to more than one student wandering off, a change of pace or a different instructional mode may be warranted. A number of strategies can be tried. A teacher could pick up the pace by putting more excitement into his or her voice, move around physically, or turn to the board to draw an example. If the focus has been on the teacher, the teacher can change the focus by asking an open-ended question. Also, teachers can physically move students around in the classroom to illustrate a point, ask students to work as a team, or form students into small problem-solving groups. It is helpful if teachers view the classroom as a laboratory and students as a primary source of energy. Anticipatory tension can help hold students' attention. A teacher's best way of using this tension is to employ variety in the teaching approach and avoid being predictable in his or her behavior.

Using Humor to Diffuse Tension

There is nothing new about this strategy. Everyone has experienced situations when a humorous comment has been able to turn a tense, anxiety-producing situation into a situation to be enjoyed or at least laughed at. Humor can clear the air and make everyone in the situation more comfortable.

A teacher with enough self-confidence to laugh at him- or herself when a situation becomes tense can defuse potential conflict situations. By adopting the adage "He who laughs at himself will never laugh alone," teachers informally demonstrate a nonabusive reaction when feeling tension in the air. A formal technique that elementary teachers can use to achieve a similar result is to verbalize a fantasy about how they would handle a situation if they were a magician. For instance, "If I were a magician, I would give you all the skills to solve this problem and help you see all the possible ways to solve any problem that ever came up." This technique is most effective if the teacher is able to make an adequate transition back to reality with a kind yet firm idea of how to attack a particular problem that many students appear to be stuck on. If the problem is social in nature, then the teacher might want to wave a magic wand and move students, call time-out, or use any number of techniques that we have discussed but played out in a magical scene. The value of humor is that humor loosens people up psychologically. When this happens, people usually are more responsive to what follows.

Providing Timely Help

Disruptive behavior does not always reflect an inner conflict. Sometimes students become frustrated by an assignment or a change in their daily routine. The student may not understand the teacher's directions or may be having difficulty with a particular part of an assignment. Instead of asking for help and exposing learning inadequacies, the student is likely to translate the feelings of frustration into some form of disruptive motor behavior, such as talking with a neighbor, drawing on the desk, or finding some interesting trinket to play with. Timely help calls for identifying the student's concern and providing needed assistance before the response to the felt frustration gets out of hand.

Restructuring the Lesson

Teachers may find it difficult to deviate from their established lesson plans. They may believe that students need to learn to adapt to demanding difficult situations and learn within the plan outlined for them. Insisting that students respond to whatever a teacher plans reflects a viewpoint that the **teachers' responsibility is to teach and the students' responsibility is to learn**. Other teachers emphasize creating conditions for learning so that their instructional plan is more process oriented. The emphasis from this perspective is not so much to teach students but to create conditions under which students are more likely to learn. This orientation leads to constantly adapting and restructuring a lesson to maximize students' learning. These teachers recognize that students have different learning styles and motivational levels and adapt lessons so students can interact with the material from a variety of perspectives. They place greater emphasis on instruction than the curriculum.

Both teaching approaches have merit. Effective teachers use elements from both. They present relevant material in systematic ways while being cognizant of students' learning styles. Effective teaching usually incorporates flexibility in the amount and rigor of material presented *and* in varying methods of delivery.

Providing Structure

Students need structure, some more structure than others. A tendency of adolescent students in particular is to test limits. When limits are not clearly defined, there is greater potential for conflict resulting from their challenging everything that is not clearly stipulated. However, if everything is stipulated, they will challenge the overall restrictive nature of their environment. This makes designing class and school rules in middle and high school particularly challenging. As discussed in the section "Permitting Behavior," when providing structure, teachers should specify which behaviors are permitted and which behaviors are not permitted. Providing structure makes contracts with students explicit enough so that they know which contracts are operative and the consequences if contracts are broken.

Appealing to Values

A frequent mistake is to intervene severely and drastically to demonstrate control over a situation. This forceful approach many times exacerbates a conflict. An alternative is to appeal to students' values. In using this approach, teachers must be aware that their own values, because of differences in culture, gender, and generations, may be different than those of their students. However, there are some values that teachers can appeal to under normal circumstances. This is only a partial list; other values specific to a community or culture also can be employed.

- Past relationships
- Real consequences
- The students' group code
- Teacher's expertise and position of responsibility

In short, thoughtful respect of values within a trusting, caring relationship among students and between students and the teacher goes a long way to ensuring the class will work and learn in harmony.

Removing Distracting Objects

It is difficult for teachers to compete with such distractions as a baseball card collection, a Walkman, and fan magazines. When a student has a flashlight, it says, "Turn me on and shine it at other students." When a student has a ball, it says, "Throw me to someone." When a student has a pea shooter, it says, "Shoot a spit wad at someone." Use of such items are usually prohibited by explicit school or classroom rules—contracts. However, students often ignore these rules or contracts. Conflicts can be avoided if items in question are quickly and quietly removed and held until the end of the school day when the disposition of these materials can be discussed. Consequences can be added, such as, if the item is brought to school again, it will be destroyed or confiscated and given to some social organization for distribution to needy children. Contracts (rules) and consequences can be planned and announced before they are needed. This makes enforcement much easier.

Time-Out

When a teacher judges that a student's behavior has reached a point where he or she does not think the student will respond to other verbal or nonverbal strategies, it may be necessary to employ **time-out**. Time-out removes students from regular classroom activities, often by separating the student from others. This approach must be used judiciously. A brief time-out might be appropriate for lower grades but not appropriate for older students.

Physical Restraint

There may be times when a student loses control and threatens him- or herself or others. In such emergencies, a student may need to be physically restrained. This strategy is recommended *only* in extreme cases and in those situations when the teacher is physically capable of controlling the situation without harm to him- or herself and the student. In all circumstances, teachers should follow administrative recommendations for handling such situations. School systems usually are governed by legal rules and regulations that must be followed in using physical restraint. Teachers should be aware of these rules and regulations and follow them carefully.

SUMMARY

In this chapter, we presented five principles useful for teachers in their quest to manage conflict. We then discussed permitting, tolerating, preventing, and interrupting strategies. We suggested the importance of understanding these strategies and outlined how and when they might be employed to manage conflict.

REFERENCES

Charles, C. M. (1992). *Building classroom discipline*. White Plains, NY: Longman.

Dreikurs, R., Grunwold, B., & Pepper, F. (1982). *Maintaining sanity in the classroom*. New York: Harper & Row.

Froyen, L. A. (1984). *Classroom management: Empowering teacher-leaders*. Upper Saddle River, NJ: Merrill/Prentice Hall.

Kameenui, E. J., & Darch, C. B. (1995). *Instructional classroom management*. White Plains, NY: Longman.

Long, N. J., & Newman, R. G. (1961, July). A differential approach to the management of surface behavior of children in schools: Teacher's handling of children in conflict. *Bulletin of the School of Education, Indiana University, 37,* 47–61.

Saaty, T. L., & Alexander, J. M. (1989). *Conflict resolution: The analytical hierarchy approach*. New York: Praeger.

Valentine, M. R. (1987). *How to deal with discipline problems in the schools*. Dubuque, IA: Kendall/Hunt.

Dealing with Multiple-Person Conflicts

Dobson and Miller (1974) discuss four potentially hazardous situations that can arise in multiple-person conflict situations. The first revolves around being a **participant-observer**. In this situation, conflict erupts between or among a number of people, while the teacher is left to observe the argument. The second, **the vise**, results in the teacher being pressured from two sides at once. Usually it begins as a disagreement between two individuals and progresses to a second stage, a joint attack on the well-intentioned teacher-mediator. The third type of conflict situation is **getting caught in the middle**, in which disagreements arise and the teacher is asked to take sides. Finally, the fourth type is the **multiple attack**, which may occur when the interaction includes two or more people verbally attacking the teacher.

PARTICIPANT-OBSERVER

This situation is the most common of the four. As students converse, their differing values, needs, learning styles, communicative styles, and goals can lead to verbally expressed conflict. Although being a participant-observer in students' conflict situations may be uncomfortable, it allows teachers to observe the process and to intervene and focus discussion on restoring harmony. Harmony will occur when teachers move students to a common ground for examining the decision or problem under discussion.

Here is an example of a teacher who is left to observe the interaction of two students. The focus of the interaction has been on a productive use of their time. The teacher has not made any recommendations but has helped the students look at various possibilities.

TEACHER: Well, we have discussed a number of options, and I'm wondering what you two would like to do.

BOB: Yes. Well, I think we ought to get others involved.

PAT: But, Bob, that is so risky! I think it would be like giving up our responsibility. Others may not want to get involved and not be committed if they did!

BOB: Well, we can't do it alone.

PAT: We worked hard to get this far. I don't want to give up on what we've started.

BOB: You sound as though the only thing you want to do is finish. You don't care how long it takes.

PAT: You seem to want to give up!

Notice that in this interchange the teacher has been on the sidelines as an observer. Besides the obvious feelings of embarrassment at watching students argue, there is the natural desire to want to help. If you do try to help, you risk getting caught in the middle or being caught in the vise and having both people vent their emotions on you. The key is to try to discover individuals' basic differences and help them focus on resolving them by using good mediation skills.

In this interchange, some value and attitudinal differences between the two on how to proceed are obvious. What is unclear is their goals. It might be assumed that their differences in values and attitudes stem from differences in goals. The teacher can test this possibility by focusing the discussion in this direction.

T: It sounds as though both of you have strong feelings about how to proceed. I'm wondering if you've discussed what you want to accomplish. It would help me if we could spend a few minutes talking about your goals. Pat, what do you want to accomplish?

PAT: What is most important to me is to get the job done in a way that I can be proud of. We set out to help kids at the elementary school and I want to finish what we started.

T: I can understand that. How about you, Bob?

BOB: Well, I figure that with both of us working we won't get done. We need help. I'd like to finish what we've started but don't think we're going to get it done on time.

T: That helps. On the surface it sounds like you have different needs, and that may be where the disagreement is coming from. I'm wondering if they are really that different, though.

PAT: What do you mean?

T: Well, one way of approaching things is to do all of the work yourself. Another is to get others involved. Both of these approaches have positive aspects and negatives to them. There might be a way to do both. Let's talk about how this might be done.

The key to helping in this form of conflict is to identify underlying themes that individuals do not seem to be dealing with directly. In the example, the teacher's hypothesis is that the students had different underlying goals. Once these are identified, appropriate strategies for resolving them can be suggested.

THE VISE

This form of conflict ultimately leads to an attack on the teacher by involved students. Despite their best efforts, teachers may find themselves caught in the vise. Let us return to the previous example and see how that might happen.

T: It sounds as though both of you have strong feelings about how to proceed. I'm wondering if you've discussed what you want to accomplish. It would help me if we could spend a few minutes talking about your goals. Pat, what do you want to accomplish?

> PAT: Of course, we've discussed our goals. We want to help kids at the elemen-
> tary school. Isn't that right, Bob?
>
> BOB: Yeah! We know what we want to accomplish and we have the same goals.

Even a teacher's best efforts may lead students to vent their emotions. The emotions usually subconsciously are intended for each other, but the teacher becomes
an easy and safe target, safe in the sense that the students will not have to deal with
their emotions with each other. When caught in a vise, the immediate goal is to
move back to the participant-observer position so that any continued attacks will be
between involved individuals. Continuing with the dialogue:

> T: There seems to be a lot of emotion tied up in this issue of how to complete
> the task you've started. Bob, tell me, how do you think you should proceed?
>
> BOB: *[still attacking]* Well, I don't think it is a matter of goals. I want to get the
> job done as fast as possible—but I want to get it done!
>
> PAT: Wait a minute, Bob! Maybe we're putting too much emphasis on speed. I
> think that what is most important is doing the job right.
>
> BOB: I'm worried about doing a good job just as much as you are, but I want to
> meet our obligation to the students.

Notice in this short interchange that the teacher did not respond directly to
attacks that put her in a vise. Rather, she directed attention to the strong emotions
being expressed and then focused back on what the students wanted to accomplish.
As Bob expressed his desires, Pat then responded to what she did not like in what
Bob said. The attack was redirected back to the *students*, and then the teacher
moved again to the participant-observer position.

At this point, the immediate goal should be to reduce conflict so that effective
problem solving can take place. The teacher's first attempt was not successful. An
effective general principle has application here: **if what you are doing is not producing what you want, try something different**. It is fairly certain that if the
teacher repeats the original response, she will probably get a repeat of the initial
reaction, an attack on her. As an example of trying something different, the teacher
might say something like the following:

> T: I guess there is a lot more emotion in this issue than I thought. Let's see if
> we can find some common ground we can agree on, and then go from
> there. One thing I heard both of you say is that you are concerned with
> doing a good job.
>
> PAT: Well, yes. That is the most important thing to me right now.
>
> BOB: Yeah, we need to accomplish what we set out to do.
>
> T: This seems to be something you both feel very strongly about. But the dif-
> ference seems to be how fast you feel you have to accomplish it.

The teacher initially used a good confluent response focused on how students were feeling. Then communication was focused on reaching a common understanding where the discussion could begin anew. Again, in multiple-conflict situations, tactics used are the same as those used in one-to-one interactions, but the focus is often on the communicative processes rather than on content itself. When strong emotion is being expressed in the communicative pattern, it is often most helpful to focus on feelings and the communication process rather than on defending oneself.

GETTING CAUGHT IN THE MIDDLE

This form of conflict occurs when the teacher is asked to take sides on an issue. Intuitively, most teachers know that if they take sides, they will be used to convince others how to think or act. They may also alienate one of the individuals. This situation usually begins with each individual trying to draw the teacher into his or her way of thinking. The teacher probably would get the feeling of being pulled in two different directions at once. For example:

BOB: I think that we should get done as fast as possible.

PAT: But if we do that, we won't do as good a job as if we take our time.

In this interchange, both students express their opinions, each in a different direction. At this point, there probably will not be a direct overture for agreement from the teacher. However, if the teacher watches nonverbal behavior closely, usually some indirect bid for agreement will be apparent: looking at the teacher while making a point, for example, nodding as a form of asking for a yes from the teacher, or gesturing toward the teacher when speaking. It is important that teachers refrain from responding verbally or nonverbally to these indirect bids. Any kind of response, such as a nod that is intended to mean "I understand you," can be taken as agreement. If the teacher does not react nonverbally to bids for agreement, something like the following might occur:

BOB: Well, Mrs. Roberts [the teacher] knows that I'm right, because by getting done as fast as we can, we can get on to other projects.

At this point, the teacher has a direct bid for agreement. She is being caught in the middle, by being asked to take sides. Her first move should be to move toward the participant-observer position.

T: You both seem to have strong opinions on how to accomplish your goals. It sounds to me as though you, Pat, place high importance on doing an excellent job and you, Bob, would like to do a good job but also are anxious to get it done.

BOB: Well, if we don't move along, we'll be at this thing forever.

PAT: But if we move too fast, we'll jeopardize quality.

T: I'm wondering what you think about other ways of maintaining quality *while* speeding up the process.

In the first response, the teacher focused again on the process and feelings being expressed. Notice that the response slowed conflict and moved the teacher back to the participant-observer position. She could then focus on underlying themes of "quality and time" as a basis for moving to resolve conflict.

A second form of getting caught in the middle can occur when two people give a third person contradictory advice. One may suggest one course of action, while the other suggests something entirely different. At this point, the student might not know which way to turn.

Teachers may experience this form of getting caught in the middle when students come for another opinion. Frequently, students will attempt to have the teacher decide for them. The teacher may offer advice that agrees with one of the two previously consulted individuals or advice that is completely different. In either case, we recommend that teachers move to the participant-observer role and help students resolve their own conflicts. For example:

SUSAN: I talked with my math teacher and a counselor, and they tell me different things. One told me that I was better off taking geometry as a sophomore, and the other said I should wait until I was a junior. Which do you think is better?

T: It can be very confusing trying to figure out which way to go, and those two options are both possible. Have you figured out the advantages of each?

Here the teacher effectively sidestepped getting caught in the middle by focusing on the student's feelings, and then he redirected communication to the student's responsibility for logically examining the situation. In this example, the student is being asked to evaluate the options as a basis for future decision making. The teacher moved to the participant-observer role and attempted to facilitate the student's problem solving. He avoided making the decision for the student or adding a third alternative; both actions could make the situation more confusing.

Again, the best approach usually is to move to the participant-observer position from which you can facilitate decision making and problem solving. Sometimes, however, students will ask for your opinion, and you may get caught in the middle without knowing it.

SUSAN: Which do you think is better, taking geometry as a sophomore or as a junior?

In this situation, the student does not explain that she has been out shopping for opinions. However, a similar response to the previous one would work equally well and avoid potential conflicts.

THE MULTIPLE ATTACK

This conflict situation occurs when the teacher is attacked by three or more people at the same time. It can occur when making a presentation to a group of students, parents, or staff members, presenting ideas in a seminar setting, or even in making a presentation to a group of colleagues. As with the other forms of conflict, the first response should be directed at moving to the participant-observer position. In this position, if the conflict continues, it will occur among participants rather than be directed at you. From this participant-observer position, you can redirect attacks to underlying themes and move discussion toward a common ground of understanding.

As an example of this process, consider the following situation in which teachers are discussing various forms of evaluation at a faculty meeting.

T1:   One of the best ways of evaluating is to have students evaluate themselves.

T2:   What do you mean let them evaluate themselves? They will all say they are the best thing since peanut butter. Then where are you?

T3:   Yeah! From what I read, you should get their peers to evaluate them. They'll at least be honest.

T4:   Yeah, she's right! Or do it yourself!

It should be obvious in this situation that our harried teacher 1 is being attacked by three people, all with personal needs. If teacher 1 agrees with any of the three, he immediately will be attacked by the other two. To avoid this and to place himself in a position where he can be most helpful to the *entire* group, he should move to the participant-observer position and redirect participant energies to underlying emotions and issues.

T1:   I can see that you all have definite opinions about what might be best. That's good, but it would be helpful to me to understand your points of view better. John, you seem to believe that people won't be up-front with their evaluations. Why don't you share with Betty and Susan why you think that is so important.

Teacher 1 has set the stage for getting the other three teachers to talk directly to one another and has provided himself an opportunity to step back into a participant-observer role. From there he can respond to "group" needs and direct the flow of communication.

ANOTHER LOOK AT THE CHAPTER 1 EXAMPLE

It is Parents' Night at school in early October. A sixth-grade teacher, Mr. Rich, begins to address a room full of parents, when a parent stands up and begins to criticize him because of his teaching style and classroom organization. The parent is obviously very upset, and the criticism revolves around the modern methods that Mr. Rich has been using. The parent wants Mr. Rich to return to the basics and stop the fancy stuff. By noticing the head nods of other parents, Mr. Rich realizes that some parents share similar feelings. Other parents remain silent. Still others seem embarrassed by this one parent's outburst.

This is a multiple-attack situation. In aikido and most martial arts, the objective in multiple attacks is to deal with one person at a time and place that person between yourself and the other attackers or to create a situation so that the other attackers begin fighting among themselves. Mr. Rich can accomplish this by first responding confluently with the parent's outburst and then by refocusing the direction of the attack.

MR. RICH: You sound very concerned about what and how your child is learning in my class. I appreciate that. I'm wondering if everyone here agrees with you.

PARENT 2:   Well, I'm concerned about what and how my child is learning too, but I don't agree with what has been said. For the first time in grade school, my child is coming home excited about school.

Several other parents nonverbally and verbally agree by saying yes. The teacher turns to the first parent who made the original attack:

MR. RICH: I'm wondering what you think about their comments?

The discussion continues among the parents who take sides for and against Mr. Rich's classroom organization. Mr. Rich remains as a participant-observer facilitating the discussion. In this example, the teacher has put the original attacker between himself and the other parents in the room and has refocused the direction of attack and conflict to be among the parents rather than focused on himself.

SUMMARY

This chapter shares the belief that you, as a teacher, must be able to help students and others see ways of resolving conflicts and be prepared to focus on the process of communication. We believe that you will be most helpful to everyone in a multiple-person conflict if you can move to and adopt the role of participant-observer and control the process of communication.

RESOURCES

Anderson, K. (1994). *Getting what you want*. New York: Penguin.

Crum, T. F. (1987). *The magic of conflict*. New York: Simon & Schuster.

Dawson, R. (1992). *Secrets of power persuasion*. Upper Saddle River, NJ: Prentice Hall.

Dobson, T., & Miller, V. J. (1974). *Giving in to get your way*. New York: Delacourt.

Markova, D. (1991). *The art of the possible*. Emeryville, CA: Conari.

Rusk, T. (1992). *The power of ethical persuasion*. New York: Penguin.

Saotome, M. (1985). *Aikido and the harmony of nature*. Boulogne, France: SEDIREP.

Westbrook, A., & Ratti, O. (1970). *Aikido and the dynamic sphere*. Rutland, VE: Tuttle.

CHAPTER 10

Mediating Conflicts

Teachers may be asked or required to mediate conflict situations. Generally, when teachers mediate conflicts, it is between students. However, teachers may be asked to mediate conflicts between a student and another teacher, between two teachers, between students and an administrator, between teachers and administrators, or between students and their parents. Mediators are neutral third parties. They do not take sides but serve as impartial listeners who facilitate communication and direct problem-solving processes between two or more persons to help restore harmony. Mediation is a diplomatic intervention to help settle differences by consent or invitation of the parties in conflict. The focus of mediation is to redirect energy of adversaries toward becoming cooperative partners in finding a mutually agreeable solution to the source of the conflict. Persons in conflict may not like one another any more than before mediation, but they should have learned how to deal with conflicts in a more harmonious manner as a result of mediation.

THE MEDIATION PROCESS

Under normal circumstances, mediation is based on the assumption that participants voluntarily agree to have a third party help them resolve their conflict. However, sometimes mediation is required by an outside authority or can be strongly suggested by a concerned person who sees the need for mediation.

Mediation entails a number of principles and steps, listed here. They should not be considered as mandatory rules but rather as guidelines for effective mediation.

1. Obtain consent from the persons in conflict to mediate.
2. Take participants to a safe and private place for talking about the conflict.
3. Explain the mediation process, and obtain a commitment from participants to use the mediation process.
4. Facilitate the process.
5. Follow up to see how the agreement is working.

Each step will now be explained in detail.

Obtaining Consent to Mediate

Generally, participation in mediation should be voluntary. When people are forced to participate in mediation, it is harder to obtain commitment to proposed solutions. At first people may be unwilling to participate because they do not know what mediation involves. You can give them a short overview of the process as a way of obtaining voluntary participation. Any explanation at the beginning should focus on your impartiality, such as "I will not take sides. I will help you try to reach a mutually agreeable solution to your problem." Ask each person, "Are you willing to work out your differences with my help?"

Taking Participants to a Safe and Private Place

The environment in which mediation is to take place should be private and provide comfortable seating for all participants. A room that assures confidentiality is ideal. In the best situation, the room should have a rectangular table so seating can be arranged as shown here (*M* = the teacher or student mediator):

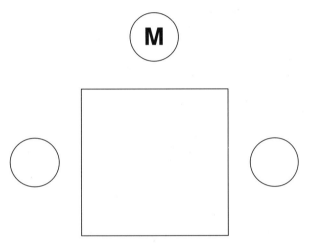

Disputants should be seated on either side of the table so they can see each other and you. Position yourself at the head of the table between parties. This seating arrangement will signify your mediating position. If you do not have a table, then seat the participants in rows facing each other with you sitting at the end similar to what is depicted here:

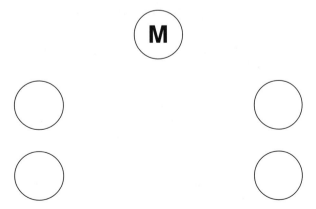

Keep the seating as equal as possible (e.g., same type and number of chairs). Do not seat disputants between yourself and the door. This position provides you the greatest psychological leverage.

Explaining the Mediation Process and Obtaining a Commitment

Several things are important to explain:

1. *The mediator's role.* Do not take sides. Your role is to facilitate communication among all parties and to help them solve the dispute in a manner that is satisfactory to everyone involved.
2. *Confidentiality.* That is, explain that whatever is said in the room will remain in the room.
3. *Rules for talking.*
   - One person speaks at a time when asked by the mediator.
   - Interruptions are not allowed.
   - Participants are to refrain from name calling.
   - All communication is to be directed to the mediator unless otherwise specified.
4. *A written agreement.* Explain that such an agreement will be developed about how each party is expected to behave at the conclusion of the mediation session.
5. *Follow-up.* Explain that you will follow up to determine the degree to which the agreement is working. Also, you will provide all parties an opportunity for another mediation session if one is needed.

A typical mediation process might flow something like the following:

1. Person 1 is asked to tell the mediator what happened while others listen.
   - *Mediator's role:* Facilitator
2. The mediator summarizes what was said or asks the other party to summarize what was said.
   - *Mediator's role:* Clarifier—Ask questions to clarify issues or actions.
3. Person 2 is asked to tell the mediator what happened while others listen.
   - *Mediator's role:* Facilitator
4. The mediator summarizes what was said or asks the other party to summarize what was said.
   - *Mediator's role:* Ask questions to clarify issues or actions.
5. The mediator helps both parties identify and express their feelings. When this is done, the mediator can direct combatants to communicate directly with each other.
   - *Mediator's role:* Facilitator
6. The mediator summarizes the two positions.
   - *Mediator's role:* Clarifier, emphasizer—Emphasize points of agreement and cite areas of disagreement. The mediator seeks agreement from participants concerning this summary.
7. Ask each participant to offer suggestions for how the conflict can be resolved. When working toward a solution, ask each participant what she or he is willing

to do to solve the problem. This can be done through brainstorming—listing every possible alternative without evaluating them. The mediator should avoid offering alternatives until combatants have exhausted all their possibilities.

- *Mediator's role:* Facilitator

8. Help participants evaluate alternatives. Some alternatives can be dismissed immediately by mutual agreement without further discussion. List positive and negative consequences of each seriously considered alternative.

   - *Mediator's role:* Facilitator, evaluator

9. With alternatives and their consequences clearly listed, help combatants work toward a solution. Sometimes a solution is obvious. At other times, additional compromise is necessary. At those times, the mediator may want to caucus with parties separately. If you caucus, meet with each party and do not reveal any caucus information from one side to the other side without permission.

   - *Mediator's role:* Negotiator

10. If no tentative agreement is reached, continue brainstorming and negotiating until an agreeable solution is found.

    - *Mediator's role:* Negotiator, problem solver

11. Be sure that all parties believe the solution is worthwhile. Make sure neither side feels pressured into accepting a solution.

    - *Mediator's role:* Facilitator

12. Seal the agreement by setting terms of the settlement in writing. The settlement should be written in the parties' own words. The settlement should state the minimum time period the solution will be in force. Have parties read, sign, and date the agreement as a way of obtaining formal commitment to implement the chosen solution. The mediator should sign the agreement as a witness.

    - *Mediator's role:* Facilitator, leader

13. Thank each party for their willingness to participate in mediation. Also, thank parties for their efforts in reaching an acceptable solution.

    - *Mediator's role:* Facilitator, leader

Following Up

Follow-up allows you to evaluate your success as a mediator and the outcome of mediation. You can talk to each participant individually, or you can arrange to meet with all participants in the mediation room again to determine how well the settlement is working.

EXAMPLE

Chapter 7 concluded with a case example in which two combating students were brought to time zero and moved toward a state of harmony. This time we will take the same situation and "subject" it to mediation.

GAIL: If you had a brain in your head, you wouldn't act so dumb.

CHRIS: You and your friends wouldn't have a brain if you put your heads together. How can you call me dumb? You've got to be halfway intelligent to know whether I have a brain, and you aren't even a half-wit.

TEACHER: Whoa! You two are about to erupt. Look, let's get out of the hall and go into my room. (Everyone moves to the teacher's room.) I would like to help you settle this so neither of you get into trouble or hurt one another. Are you willing to let me help?

GAIL: I don't know.

CHRIS: Yeah, you'll probably agree with him, anyway.

T: You can either trust me and see if we can work this through or go back to fighting until either or both of you get in trouble and possibly hurt one another.

GAIL: I'm willing to give it a try.

CHRIS: OK.

T: Here's how we will do this. If each of you would be willing to tell me your side of the story without the other interrupting, I think I can help you find a way to settle this. I won't take sides, and whatever anyone says will not leave this room. You only can talk to me, not to one another, unless I say it is OK. Before you leave the room, I will help the two of you write an agreement stating how each of you will behave when you see one another. All three of us will sign it, and 2 weeks from today we will meet here at 10:30 and see how both of you are doing. Is all of this agreeable with the two of you?

GAIL: It sounds fair enough.

CHRIS: I agree as long as what we say stays in this room.

T: I guarantee that it will.

GAIL: Who goes first?

T: You go first unless the two of you want me to flip a coin to see who goes first. Chris, do you want me to flip a coin, or is it OK if Gail goes first?

CHRIS: Go ahead.

Usually in a few minutes both sides will have exhausted the content of their disagreement. Then, you must decide whether to summarize and move on or to provide both parties further opportunity to express their feelings. It is helpful if emotions are reduced sufficiently so that they do not interfere with working on an agreement.

T: You both have said that the mere sight of the other person "sets you off." Gail, any ideas why this might be? Chris, any ideas?. . . .

T: You both mentioned that you and your friends can't stand the other's friends. So, while this seems to be the case between the two of you, it may not be. You both may be reacting the way your friends expect you to act. It's possible that because of commitments to your friends, you aren't free to reach an agreement between the two of you. Could this be?

GAIL: Maybe.

CHRIS: I hadn't thought about it, but it's possible.

T: As you can probably guess, teachers aren't going to let you fight or scream at one another. Unless you can come up with some ideas that satisfy each of you and how you will look in your friends' eyes, it's back to fighting and probably expulsion. What can you do about it? Any suggestions?

GAIL: How about if we avoid one another?

T: What do you think, Chris, can you avoid one another?

CHRIS: OK, it's worth a try.

T: Write down your class schedules, where you locker is, what hall you are in between classes, and how you move from class to class. In fact, draw a map of your day and put times on it. . . . Let's look at these maps and see when you two are likely to run into one another. . . . It appears that there are three times each day you might. Are your friends around all three times?

GAIL: Only in the morning for me.

CHRIS: Only in the afternoon for me.

T: Alright then. In the morning, Gail, you need to find a different route, and in the afternoon, Chris, you need to find a different route. What about when neither of your friends are around? Do you need to work on an alternate route on alternate days, or can you come up with a simpler solution?

GAIL: What do you mean?

T: When neither of your friends are around, you won't have to perform for them. We have a way worked out so you won't see one another in the morning and afternoon and can still be with your friends. In late morning you don't have to worry about your friends, so it might be possible to be a little more creative.

CHRIS: How about if we just don't see one another?

GAIL: How can we do that?

T: Wait Gail, you seem to be asking Chris that question instead of me. It seems like a good question and shows you are listening. So OK, what are your thoughts, Chris?

CHRIS: You know. We see one another but we ignore it—we just don't make any big deal about it.

T: Is it agreed? Different routes in the morning and afternoon and not seeing one another in late morning?

GAIL: OK.

CHRIS: Yeah.

T: OK, I've written it down as both of you have agreed. Sign here and then I'll sign. We meet 2 weeks from today, and you each can tell me if you lived up to the contract and if you think the other person has lived up to the contact. If you think it isn't going to work and you are going to go at one another before the 2 weeks are up, get in to see me. I'll decide whether we need to meet sooner than 2 weeks from now.

This process could take 5 minutes, or it could take an hour. If one of the students does not accept the idea or the process, it will not work and that is the end of it. If both students agree that it might work, you control the process and provide suggestions for working toward solutions that will resolve the conflict. In doing so, efforts should be made to solicit significant contributions from both students toward the plan of action. This will help them feel a commitment toward carrying out the plan. Also, continuous, confluent responses in your interactions with both students will model harmonious behavior and establish an interpersonal environment conducive to reducing conflict.

SUMMARY

This chapter highlighted how mediation can be accomplished. Five steps were presented and discussed. Namely, guidelines for effective mediation were to (a) obtain consent from the persons in conflict, (b) take participants to a private, safe environment for talking about the situation, (c) explain the mediation process and obtain a commitment from participants to use the process, (d) facilitate the process, and (e) follow up to assure that the plan of action is working. These five steps work best when you use confluent responses in your interactions with participants.

RESOURCES

Sorenson, D. L. (1992). *Conflict management training activities*. Minneapolis, MN: Educational Media.

Sorenson, D. L. (1992). *Conflict resolution and mediation for peer helpers*. Minneapolis, MN: Educational Media.

CHAPTER 11

Developing a Peer Mediation Program

In this chapter, we discuss peer mediation, highlight goals typical in peer mediation programs, focus on how to choose and train peer mediators, emphasize what peer mediators can learn through their participation in a peer mediation program, examine issues relevant to administration of peer mediation programs, and attend to potential trouble spots in such programs.

PEER MEDIATION

The February (1995) *NEA Today* cover story, "From Dispute to Dialogue," highlights a peer mediation program in DuVal High School in Lanham, Maryland. The staff at DuVal report that since the school's peer mediation program was initiated in 1990, suspensions for fighting have dropped dramatically, and the social climate of the school has changed for the better. Educators, parents, even students want peer programs to work. The alternative is more tension and more violence in the schools. "Right now, every hour brings 2,000 more students attacked on school grounds, 900 more teachers threatened, 40 more assaulted" (*NEA Today,* 1995, p. 11).

Peer mediation programs provide educators a resource for dealing with escalating conflict in the schools. They do this by establishing a process that teachers and students can use to work together to mediate student concerns. When properly established, peer mediation programs focus students' attention on the need for students to become part of the solution. Peer mediation programs provide a vehicle for student problem solving, decision making, and action.

Several resources provide guidance for developing peer mediation programs, all of which generally follow a few simple guidelines. In this chapter, we will discuss these guidelines and highlight a number of concerns that we believe to be important when establishing peer mediation programs. The important focal points to be discussed in designing and implementing a peer mediation program are:

- establishing goals of the peer mediation program,
- choosing peer mediators,
- training peer mediators,
- attending to the learning of peer mediators,
- administering the peer mediation program, and
- troubleshooting.

Program Goals

The school staff should agree on the reasons for establishing a peer mediation program and be supportive of the program goals. Possible goals and objectives might include the following:

- To establish a specially selected and trained group of students who will supplement and complement the school staff in promoting harmony in the school
- To provide positive peer role modeling for dealing with conflicts

- To increase and enhance cooperation among all students
- To take the initiative regarding conflict resolution. This can be done by asking peer mediators to serve as role models, prompting these students to look for problems that could develop, and offering assistance when they see a situation about to escalate.
- To alleviate stress among students when the "heat" begins to rise in a relationship and neither party can hold back without assistance
- To increase everyone's understanding of the sources of conflict in students' lives. The most common sources are breaking up with boy- or girlfriend, arguments with parent(s), trouble with a brother or sister, increased arguments between parents, changes in family circumstances, trouble with classmates, trouble with teachers, and academic difficulties.
- To provide positive peer expectations for interpersonal cooperation, not conflict

These and other goals and objectives can provide the basis for developing peer mediation programs. Since each program should prepare mediators to address school specific goals and objectives and the particular needs of students in their school, mediators must be knowledgeable regarding sources of stress and conflict among the student body.

Choosing Peer Mediators

Choosing effective peer mediators is crucial to the success of peer mediation programs. Several considerations should be kept in mind in selecting peer mediators. First, the staff will need to develop selection criteria that accommodate both student and staff values. This approach will eliminate some students from consideration because they lack student support and some faculty because as staff, they might not have the skills required to mediate. In addition, staff must be prepared to consider students who fall outside their preferred choices. For instance, students may nominate peers whom they think will be effective but who are not viewed by staff as being good students or having personal qualities that the staff values.

Second, the school staff should decide beforehand how many peer mediators are needed. A good rule of thumb is two peer mediators per classroom, one female and one male, or a ratio of one mediator to 15 to 20 students. In general, a larger pool of potential peer mediators should be identified than is needed because when these students are being trained, some may clearly not be suited for the role of peer mediator. Also, some peer mediators who are effective may decide to discontinue participating.

Once criteria for selection have been established and the number of peer mediators has been determined, selection can commence. Three methods that can be used to identify possible peer mediators are described here.

Peer Nomination

One way of recruiting peer mediators is to advertise the program and ask students to nominate other students as potential peer mediators. Peer nomination depends on a thorough explanation about peer mediation and the peer mediator's role. When soliciting nominations, specify the positive attributes required of individuals being sought. Some students will be both popular and natural mediators. If students do not understand the necessary characteristics of a peer mediator, the risk increases that peer nominations will not result in effective students being nominated. Students doing the nominating should be cautioned to nominate individuals whose judgment they respect and to refrain from viewing the nominating process as a popularity contest.

Self-Nomination

Students can be encouraged to apply to become peer mediators. We recommend several steps if this process is used. Students should complete an application that might include the following:

- The applicant's perception of a peer mediator's role and a self-assessment regarding their capabilities to fulfill the role. This could be provided through a written statement, an interview, or a combination of the two.
- A guardian or parent's signature. This will indicate that students have communicated with their guardian or parent about their desire to participate and that their guardian or parent approves of their participation.
- A form on which students provide evidence of others' support of their application. Usually, support from five students and faculty is viewed as being sufficient.

Staff Nomination

Some schools develop peer mediation programs by having staff members nominate potential peer mediators. Once staff understand the peer mediation program and needed qualities and skills of peer mediators, they are able to nominate students who can mediate effectively.

Interview Panel

Usually, whether peer nominations, self-nominations, or staff recommendations are used to generate a list of possible peer mediator candidates, an interview panel will need to be organized to make final selections. Membership on the committee should include representatives of the student body who will be in the majority and a minority consisting of faculty, administrators, and staff. The majority of the selection team should be students since candidates are going to be student peer mediators. Typical peer mediator qualities include but are not limited to the following:

- The ability to remain calm under stress in a conflict situation
- Good listening skills
- An ability to make a group presentation. Sometimes peer mediators may be required to make classroom presentations regarding the peer mediation program and to explain the mediation process to several combatants at the beginning of the mediation process.

- An ability to relate to many different personalities with different problems
- Dependability in meeting responsibilities
- An ability to express their views about situations. Failure to do so may add to the conflict or appear to favor one side over the other.
- Self-confidence with healthy self-esteem. Sometimes both parties in a conflict turn on the mediator, and the mediator must be able to react strongly and assuredly.
- An open and outgoing personality. Shy people will not be in control of the mediation process or be able to assert themselves when it is necessary.

Such qualities and skills generally are necessary to be an effective peer mediator. However, each school must decide on the qualities and skills necessary to meet particular student needs within their school.

Once an interview panel has been established, procedures for how the panel will operate must be established, guidelines for interviewing candidates developed, and panel members trained to interview candidates. The training of peer mediators includes practice in interviewing and learning to anticipate and respond to typical questions and situations peer mediators encounter.

Training Peer Mediators

Peer mediation training programs take a variety of forms and can be conducted by different school staff members. Very often, because of the skills necessary for peer mediation in a particular school, school counselors are involved in the training programs. Peer mediation training involves teaching facilitative skills and attitudes as well as teaching mediators how to process their own feelings and to seek assistance from others when needed. Most programs provide peer mediators training in these areas:

- Understanding how students and mediators can have differing perceptions of an event
- How to help students describe their perceptions in an understandable manner
- Listening skills, including restating, paraphrasing, and summarizing
- Problem-solving and goal-setting skills
- The mediation process

If training is effective, peer mediators should be able to do the following at the conclusion of their training:

1. Describe the essence of a conflict in one or two sentences.
2. Identify the relationship (e.g. family, friends) between and among combatants.
3. Identify the needs or goals of involved parties.
4. Understand what winning and losing means to both sides.
5. Discover past relationships of combatants.
6. Recognize which aspects of their involvement helped resolve the conflict.

7. Describe the outcome of the resolution process.

8. Describe how the outcome could have been improved.

9. Describe how the mediation process could have moved faster.

10. Know whether the problem or conflict is resolved.

Skills can be taught to peer mediators in several ways. A brief discussion of these follows.

Some schools arrange for peer mediators to receive training outside the school setting. This can occur before the start of the school year, after school, on weekends, or for a few concentrated days while school is in session. Usually 3 or 4 days of intensive training is required. Initial training is frequently supplemented with ongoing, case-specific training that can be scheduled as needed or at regularly scheduled intervals.

An immediate result of being taken off campus for peer mediation training is to establish that both the training and mediators are special. This effect can serve to enhance the peer mediators' potential influence when they engage in the mediation process.

A school system may elect to provide peer mediation training during the school day. When done this way, training can extend over several weeks. Because most students' schedules are very full and missing classes is a problem for students and faculty alike, it may be difficult to find sufficient training time during the normal school day to train all peer mediators at one time. Therefore, trainers may need to find creative ways to train students. Approaches that some schools have found to be successful include training peer mediators individually, teaching students how to train other students, providing students peer mediation training tapes, and giving students written materials that describe the process.

Trainers will likely be faced with finding sufficient time to conduct the peer mediation training. Trainers in this situation should keep in mind, in addition to the prior considerations, that the techniques used by peer mediators are less important than the mediators' sensitivity and problem-solving capabilities. One way to help ensure the adequacy of peer mediators' knowledge, sensitivity, and skill is by using various self-monitoring tools. Self-monitoring skills can be developed by teaching mediators to use a disputant's evaluation form or a mediator report form such as that described here:

Disputants' Questions

1. Do you feel the mediator listened to you?

2. Was the mediator fair (did not take sides)?

3. Were you satisfied with the resolution? Do you think the other person(s) were as satisfied as you?

What Peer Mediators Learn

Peer mediators learn several skills and attitudes that are basic to succeeding in most human endeavors. Peer mediation training benefits students by teaching attitudes

Student Mediator Report Form

Mediator's name: _____ Date: _____

Students involved in the conflict: _____

_____

Type of conflict: _____ Argument

_____ Fight

_____ Gossip/rumor affecting someone's reputation

Referred by: _____ Student _____ Teacher _____ Administrator

_____ Counselor _____ Yourself _____ Parent

_____ Other school staff _____

The mediation began (time/date) _____ and ended _____

Was the conflict resolved? Yes _____ No _____ Inconclusive _____

If resolved, is there a written agreement? _____

Mediator evaluation:

What did you do well? _____

What needs more practice? _____

Was the agreement a good one? Why?_____

_____

Mediator's signature: _____

Figure 11–1
Student Mediator Report Form

and skills that carry over into their relationships with friends, family, teachers, and others. Mediators learn assertive communication skills that can serve them throughout life. These skills suggest that peer mediation may be limited to students who developmentally have achieved the capability to think inferentially—rarely evidenced in the primary grades and only occasionally in the intermediate grades. An overview of these skills and attitudes follows.

Being Nonjudgmental

The mediator is asked to withhold judgment regarding fairness, equity, and even appropriateness of an agreement reached by two combatants. This requires the mediator to withhold verbal and nonverbal judgments. It is important for mediators to learn to maintain a "poker face" throughout the mediation process.

Being Flexible

The mediator sets the stage but then has to let participants choose the pace and direction of communication. The mediator's task is to help participants stay within mediation guidelines. Flexibility is important to assure that the mediator's behavior is viewed as being unbiased, nonjudgmental, and facilitative.

Being Nondefensive

The mediator has to enforce rules of mediation. By enforcing the rules, the mediator may become the object of one or both parties' hostility. If the mediator responds defensively and aggressively, then he or she can be drawn into the dispute. This could escalate the present dispute or serve as a foundation for a new dispute.

Being Patient

Mediation requires that the mediator gently nudge students when they get bogged down or when they get off on tangents. The temptation to step in and offer a solution, particularly when the mediator has helped resolve similar disputes, is tempting. This temptation must be resisted. Also, the mediator must avoid acting bored, appearing to be waiting impatiently for the two sides to have their say without really listening, or failing to attend to what and how something is being said. The mediator must stay mentally alert and patient although not necessarily verbally involved.

Being an Effective Listener

Mediators have to be proficient using six active listening techniques. First, mediators must know how to **encourage** both parties to keep talking. This is done without agreeing or disagreeing, by using neutral phrases such as, "Can you tell me more?" Next, they must be able to **clarify** what is being said. This will minimize misunderstanding primarily by restating wrong interpretations. It can be used to pressure the speaker to explain further, as exemplified by "When did this happen?" Third, by **restating** what has been said, mediators can demonstrate that they are listening and want to understand. An example is "So you would like John to trust you more, is that it?" Fourth, **summarizing** serves to review progress, pull important ideas together, and be the basis for further discussion. An example would be "This seems to be what you have agreed is important to do next." A fifth technique is through **validating** the worthiness of both parties to the dispute. This can be done by acknowledging and reinforcing the value of how both sides view the issue and how they have worked out a solution. A validating comment would sound something like, "I appreciate your willingness to work this through and agreeing as to what can be done." The sixth active listening technique, **reflecting**, requires more training than most peer mediation programs provide. When using reflection, the mediator is asked to demonstrate an understanding of how combatants feel or to help them explore and evaluate their feelings. Reflective statements are relatively easy to make: "You seem very upset or very angry." The question is, are these statements accurate, and is the combatant ready to hear someone describe how they feel? Reflecting feelings is an important aspect of mediation. However, it must be used carefully, after extensive training and supervision.

Being Imaginative

Mediators are expected to "add something" when the process bogs down and people begin to repeat themselves. They are expected to assist the parties to look at things in a different way or from a different perspective. It is important that mediators keep an open mind and attempt to find creative solutions, ones that can help participants identify possibilities for resolution or compromise.

Being Forceful and Persuasive

Mediators can guide the mediation process by questioning and summarizing. They need to demonstrate being assertive without being aggressive. By modeling assertiveness, mediators provide combatants a model for behaving toward one another. Modeling assertive behavior can become part of the solution. Rules governing assertive conversation are relatively simple. The mediator can use an "I" message to define the problem situation to describe what he or she has observed. Mediators must learn how to feel and act comfortably while being assertive. When they can demonstrate this ability, they will model how one can feel and act in an effective yet nonaggressive manner. Frequently, mediator modeling elicits similar responses from adversaries.

Administering a Peer Mediation Program

Ideally, a mediation room will be established that has characteristics similar to those outlined in Chapter 10. Also, one staff member should be assigned the responsibility for organization and day-to-day administration of the peer mediation program. While administration of a peer mediation program has to be designed to meet the needs of students in a specific school environment, some general administrative guidelines can be considered.

1. Develop a "Request for Peer Mediation" form and establish a secure place where these forms can be obtained and deposited by interested students. This is important so that when students or staff feel that mediation is necessary to resolve conflicts, the form to initiate the process and a secure, confidential arrangement for

submission will be available. Very often secured boxes are located where they are easily accessible to students and teachers. A referral form might ask for information like that presented in Figure 11–2.

    2.   In some schools, peer mediators are identified by special badges or identification tags. By identifying mediators, students know who can be appealed to for mediation relative to conflicts that they are experiencing or witnessing.

    3.   The person(s) organizing and administering the peer mediation program should have training in the basic skills and processes needed for mediation and should be available for consultation to peer mediators.

Troubleshooting

Although one of the primary rules for effective conflict mediation is that what is discussed in the mediation room remain confidential, staff members who coordinate the peer mediation program need to monitor the program to ensure success. A peer mediation program can be monitored in several ways.

- By keeping track of the number of students and staff who avail themselves of the peer mediation program
- By interviewing students and staff who have taken advantage of the peer mediation program. Interviews should focus on participants' feelings and thoughts about the program, not on the nature of their conflict. Asking the same three questions in an interview as asked in the disputants' questionnaire described earlier may elicit somewhat different answers. Interviews provide an opportunity for students to expand, elaborate, or alter their responses.
- By periodically distributing an anonymous questionnaire to the student body to ask them about their reactions to the peer mediation program

---

Referral for Peer Mediation

Date :_____ Your name/relationship to those involved: _____

Names of those involved:_____

Where did the conflict occur?_____

Note: You may request a mediator for yourself if you are having a conflict or request mediation for other students whom you would like to see reach a peaceful resolution to a conflict.

Figure 11–2
Referral Form for Peer Mediation

Systematically collecting information about the peer mediation program will allow administrators and consultants to make adjustments when needed. Adjustments may take many forms. The general organization of the program may need to be altered, including changes in the forms, referral procedures, selection process, the number of available peer mediators, or recruitment of mediators for a more diverse group. Peer mediators also may require additional training or be provided more support and access to consultants. The manner in which the peer mediation program is advertised and marketed may need to be changed as well. Making necessary corrections will not be possible without systematically collecting information about the program.

SUMMARY

In this chapter, we provided an outline for developing and administering a peer mediation program, with examples and principles to keep in mind while developing such a program. These principles are organized in five main categories:

Goals of a peer mediation program

Choosing peer mediators

Training peer mediators

Administering a peer mediation program

Troubleshooting

REFERENCE

NEA Today. (1995, February). *From dispute to dialogue,* p. 11.

ADDITIONAL RESOURCES

Albuquerque Mediation Center. (1986). *Lessons in conflict resolution: Grades 4–6.* Albuquerque, NM: Author. (1500 Walter SE, Albuquerque, NM 87102)

Alexander, E. R. (1979). *The reduction of cognitive conflict. Journal of Conflict Resolution, 23*(1), 120–138.

Auvine, B. (1977). *A manual for group facilitators,* Madison, WI: Center for Conflict Resolution.

Beer, J. (Ed.) (1982). *Mediator's handbook: Peacemaking in your neighborhood.* Concordville, PA: Friends Suburban Project.

Burnett, E. C., & Daniels, J. (1985). The impact of family of origin and stress on interpersonal conflict resolution skills in young adult men. *American Mental Health Counselors Association Journal, 7*(4), 162–171.

Community Board Program, Inc. (1992). *Starting a conflict managers program.* San Francisco: Author.

Cowan, D., Palomares, S., & Schilling, D. (1992). *Teaching the skills of conflict resolution.* Spring Valley, CA: Innerchoice.

Crum, T. F. (1987). *The magic of conflict.* New York: Simon & Schuster.

Crum, T., & Warner, J. (1994). *Your conflict cookbook: A teacher's handbook for helping students deal with anger and conflict.* Victor, NY: Aiki Works.

Deutsch, M. (1973). *The resolution of conflict: Constructive and destructive processes.* New Haven, CT: Yale University Press.

Dobson, T., & Miller, V. J. (1994). *Aikido in everyday life: Giving in to get your way.* Grand Isle, VT: Softpower.

Drew, N. (1987). *Learning the skills of peacemaking.* Rolling Hills Estates, CA: Jalmar.

Filley, A. C. (1975). *Interpersonal resolution,* Glenview, IL: Scott, Foresman.

Fletcher, R. (1986). *Teaching peace: Skills for living in a global society.* New York: Harper & Row.

Folberg, J., & Taylor, A. (1984). *Mediation.* San Francisco: Jossey-Bass.

Folger, J. P., & Poole, M. S. (1984). *Working through conflict: A communication perspective,* Glenview, IL: Scott, Foresman.

Foster, E. S. (1989). *Tutoring: Learning by helping* (rev. ed.). Minneapolis, MN: Educational Media.

Hazouri, S. P., & McLaughlin, M. S. (1991). *Peer listening in middle school: Training activities for students.* Minneapolis, MN: Educational Media.

Johnson, D. W., & Johnson, R. T. (1991). *Teaching students to be peacemakers.* Minneapolis, MN: Interaction.

Judson, S. (1984). *A manual on non-violence and children.* Philadelphia: New Society.

Kolb, D. M., & Glidden, P. A. (1986). Getting to know your conflict options: Using conflict as a creative force. *Personnel Administrator, 31,* 77–88.

Kreidler, W. J. (1984). *Creative conflict resolution: More than 200 activities for keeping peace in the classroom.* Glenview, IL: Scott Foresman.

Kressell, K., & Pruitt, D. (1989). *Mediation research.* San Francisco: Jossey-Bass.

Lehr, J. B., & Martin, C. (1992). *We're all at risk: Inviting learning for everyone.* Minneapolis, MN: Educational Media.

McLaughlin, M. S., & Hazouri, S. P. (1992). *T*L*C, tutoring, leading, cooperating: Training activities for elementary school students.* Minneapolis, MN: Educational Media.

McLaughlin, M. S., & Hazouri, S. P. (1994). *The race for safe schools: A staff development curriculum.* Minneapolis, MN: Educational Media.

Moore, C. (1986). *The mediation process.* San Francisco: Jossey-Bass.

Putman, L. L. (1988). Communication and interpersonal conflict in organizations. *Management Communication Quarterly, 1,*(3), 293–301.

Reardon, B. A. (1988). *Educating for global responsibility: Teacher-designed curricula for peace education K–12.* New York: Teachers College Press, Columbia University.

Sadalla, G., Henriquez, M., & Holmberg, M. (1990). *Conflict resolution: An elementary school curriculum.* San Francisco: Community Board Program.

Sadalla, G., Henriquez, M., & Holmberg, M. (1990). *Conflict resolution: A secondary curriculum.* San Francisco: Community Board Program.

Schmidt, F. (1994). *Mediation: Getting to win!* Miami: Grace Contrino Abrams Peace Education Foundation.

Schmidt, F., & Friedman, A. (1990). *Creative conflict solving for kids.* Miami: Grace Contrino Abrams Peace Education Foundation.

Schmidt, F., & Friedman, A. (1990). *Fighting fair: Dr. Martin Luther King, Jr., for kids.* Miami: Grace Contrino Abrams Peace Education Foundation.

Schmidt, F., & Friedman, A. (1990). *Peace-making skills for little kids.* Miami: Grace Contrino Abrams Peace Education Foundation.

Schniedewind, N., & Davidson, E. (1987). *Cooperative learning, cooperative lives: A source book of learning activities for building a peaceful world.* Dubuque, IA: Brown.

Schrumpf, F., Crawford, D., & Usadel, H. C. (1991). *Peer mediation: Conflict resolution in schools [student manual and program guide].* Champaign, IL: Research Press.

Sorenson, D. L (1992). *Conflict management training activities.* Minneapolis, MN: Educational Media.

Sorenson, D. L (1992). *Conflict resolution and mediation for peer helpers.* Minneapolis, MN: Educational Media.

Tjpsvold, D., & Johnson, D. W. (1989). *Productive conflict management.* Edina, MN: Interaction.

Webster-Doyle, T. (1990). *Tug of war: Peace through understanding conflict.* Middlebury, VT: Atrium Society.

Webster-Doyle, T. (1991). *Why is everybody picking on me?* Middlebury, VT: Atrium Society.

CHAPTER 12

Getting the Most Out of Your Students

This text was written to address issues of classroom conflict management. It is appropriate to end this discussion by focusing on proactive approaches that can dramatically affect students and channel them toward positive interactions in school. The aikido principles of blending, joining, unbalancing, and redirecting discussed in Chapter 1 and the confluent response detailed in Chapter 6 can be used for preventing conflict as well as managing it. Teachers can be a positive, proactive force, a force so powerful that conflict can be preempted before it begins. Teachers literally can create a positive environment that will prevent conflict from occurring. They can do this by **focusing on students**, **focusing on their approach**, **using feedback effectively**, and **using the power of groups**.

FOCUSING ON STUDENTS

An effective way to manage conflict is to prevent it from occurring. One of the best ways to do this is to focus on students in a way that builds their self-confidence and self-worth. Students who feel good about themselves and value their social environment are less likely to act out, become distraught, and incite or participate in conflict situations. Described here are five process principles for helping students to achieve and maintain a positive attitude, an attitude that can prevent conflict from occurring. These process principles are an application of the aikido principles of blending with and joining students' energies to promote positive growth.

Expect the Best from Your Students

Rosenthal and Jacobson (1968), in *Pygmalion in the Classroom,* demonstrated that teachers' expectations about their students' intelligence appeared to bring about changes in the students' intelligence test scores and classroom achievement. Some teachers were told that their students all had above-average intelligence test scores despite their real scores, which were average. Other teachers were told that their students had average intelligence test scores. Students in the classrooms in which teachers were told that they were above average achieved above-average scores on further intelligence tests and demonstrated above-average achievement. Students in classrooms in which teachers thought that they had average students tested and achieved at average levels. When teachers expected more and demonstrated their expectations, students responded positively. They accomplished more.

The Pygmalion effect can be extended beyond academic accomplishment. The impact of positive teacher expectations can be widespread. Usually, students respond to positive expectations with positive behavior, positive attitudes toward learning and classroom involvement, reduced incidence of conflict, and more positive interpersonal interactions. By contrast, negative teacher expectations are frequently followed by negative student behaviors, poor attitudes toward learning, increased conflict, and troubled interpersonal interactions. The long-term impact when teachers adopt a positive perspective is student involvement and a positive classroom environment. When conflict occurs in this environment, it is usually short-lived and low-intensity.

Focus on Strengths Rather Than Weaknesses

By focusing on strengths instead of weaknesses, you can help students build positive self-concepts, self-esteem, and a sense of self-efficacy (Gladding, 1996). Students need to feel a sense of self-worth, a sense that they are secure, and are valued. Muro and Kottman (1995) suggest that "absence of this sense of worth may cause individuals to engage in self-defeating behaviors" (p. 129), behaviors that can lead to conflict.

Young (1992) identifies a number of effective interventions that counselors can use to focus on students' strengths. These interventions also can be used in the classroom. He suggests (a) acknowledging students' efforts and improvements, (b) concentrating on capacities and possibilities rather than on past failures, (c) focusing on strengths, and (d) showing faith in students' competencies and capabilities (p. 237). All four interventions are positive and forward looking versus negative and oriented toward past behaviors. When teachers apply Young's perspective and focus on students' strengths, students learn to view themselves in a positive light. They learn that they are valued and worthwhile, and their actions are likely to be positive and less likely to be destructive and conflict producing.

Help Students Discover Their Hidden Talents

Teachers can help students acknowledge and use their talents. Consider the following case: John, a 10th-grade student, transferred into Mrs. Cautella's class toward the end of the first semester. John did not know anybody and consequently felt quite lonely. Mrs. Cautella was sensitive to John's plight and actively worked to overcome it. She made it a point to get to know John and encourage him to become involved in classroom activities. In her discussions with John, Mrs. Cautella discovered that he was bilingual. She used this knowledge to involve John in a peer tutoring program in which John, along with other students from the class, tutored children in the adjacent elementary school. John's unique bilingual skill was a bonus to the program. He was recognized for his skill, involved with other 10th graders in providing a service, and, in a short time, was fully accepted by his classmates.

Although John probably would have been accepted by his classmates anyway, by being involved in the tutoring program he demonstrated a similarity to his classmates, a commitment to being helpful, and a willingness to extend himself. Involvement provided John a means for demonstrating his unique bilingual talent and for becoming *actively* involved with his classmates. This shortened the amount of time needed to be accepted.

By helping students use their talents, teachers can foster students' self-confidence. This confidence usually results in happier students. These students usually feel good about themselves, are more open to feedback, and are less likely to act out to get attention.

Capitalize on Students' Desire to Succeed

Success is nicer than failure. Most people would agree with this simple statement. Students are no different. Most students would rather succeed than fail. Teachers can use this simple truth to help students accomplish their goals in a personally satisfying way. Young (1992) believes that this can be done by focusing on things that excite or interest students, confronting discouraging beliefs, lending enthusiasm to what interests students, and fostering commitment toward goals (p. 237). When teachers vocally and forcefully focus on things that excite or interest students, they provide an encouraging force that will tend to foster achievement. It is through their enthusiasm that teachers can help students to overcome moments when they lose sight of their goals or get discouraged. Honest, intense, encouraging communication by teachers can help students accomplish their goals by activating their desire to succeed, promoting their personal and academic self-worth, and helping them overcome their fears and/or self-doubts.

A result of promoting student success is less classroom conflict. Typically, successful students become model students. Students who are successful and enjoy the educational process usually do not involve themselves in, promote, or encourage conflict.

Refrain from Using Competition as a Primary Motivator

Although American society is reputed to be highly competitive, not all people in the United States are motivated by this dynamic force. As discussed in Chapter 2, Hall (1981) suggests that individuals from diverse subcultures react to competitive situations in different ways at different times or in different situations. For many people, competition is debilitating. For example, a student who is unsure of herself could be discouraged by comparison with others. Comparison or competition with others could prevent the student from trying. It might be psychologically easier for the student not to try and fail than to compete actively and not succeed. Motivation by competition works with some but fails with many. Competition does not model the necessary cooperation people need in the work world.

If competition is not used as a motivating factor, what might teachers use? McGinnes (1985) offers a common approach used by many motivators. That is, tailor the motivator to the person. Know what motivates the individual. To do this, teachers must gain an in-depth knowledge of each student. For some, encouragement will be the prime motivator. For others, praise, caring, involvement, or fear might work better. For still others, competition might be the key. Tracey (1990) broadens the discussion of motivation by suggesting that motivation is directly related to one's sense of personal power. By raising students' responsibility for what is done and how it is accomplished; increasing students' knowledge and information; providing accurate, pertinent, and timely feedback; and extending overriding respect, teachers can increase students' power to make and act on personally meaningful decisions.

Understanding and involvement appear to be the key ingredients. Teachers can foster motivation by recognizing and acting on student differences and trusting students to be responsible for their actions. For this approach to be successful, however, teachers must recognize that students may have failures. That is, success is not guaranteed. When students are allowed to be responsible for their actions, it is conceivable that, at times, they will be unsuccessful. Long-term motivation is enhanced when teachers view short-term failure as being learning experiences, experiences that can serve as reference points for change, growth, and eventual success.

From a conflict management perspective, the advantage of motivating students by empowering them is they will feel responsible for what happens to them. This sense of responsibility typically inhibits students from blaming others for what happens to them and discourages students from striking out at others for their failures. When students are empowered in a caring environment, they work to maintain the environment. This positive desire to maintain the environment is a powerful force that inhibits students' desire to behave in ways that lead to conflict.

FOCUSING YOUR APPROACH

In addition to focusing on students, teachers can foster positive classroom attitudes by focusing their approach to teaching. Although many issues could be discussed under the general category of teaching approach, we have selected four principles of particular importance to be used as a stimulus for generating others. Described here are some teaching process principles incorporating the aikido principle of unbalancing.

Establish High Standards of Excellence

There are formal and informal expectations that all students will achieve. Although this is a laudable belief, many forces interfere with its realization—for example, poverty, drugs, uninterested parents, poor learning environments, negative peer pressure, insufficient funding, unprepared teachers, and unmotivated students. At times, when positive expectations come face to face with these negative forces, the illusion of doing well is substituted for actual achievement. This can occur in many ways, but one of the primary ways is for teachers to reduce expectations. This shift results in higher grades by students and the illusion that students are doing well. One recently interviewed teacher called this the "success for all, learning for none" syndrome. Temporarily, students feel good about themselves, parents are happy, administrators are proud of their teachers, and teachers believe that they have been successful. In the long term, creation of this illusion is problematic. Students do not learn what they need to know. They fail to acquire skills and knowledge needed for true understanding and do not gain an adequate foundation for subsequent courses. In addition, students are not provided an opportunity to experience the joy of success that can be gained through their own hard work.

Obviously, most teachers do not approach teaching from this perspective. Most are willing to set high standards and push, pull, hound, tease, and/or inspire students to learn and succeed. This approach is frequently difficult, frustrating, and lonely. Teachers may not sense support for adopting this perspective from parents, administrators, or, in some cases, fellow teachers. They may have to consciously resist temptation to take the easy road. When teachers set high standards and resist pressure to do otherwise, students are the benefactors. Students learn that their mental efforts can produce results and that they can accomplish difficult tasks. In addition to acquiring foundational material, they gain confidence in their ability to learn. Finally, when teachers set high standards, successful students develop a sense of pride in themselves. Frequently, students feel good that they were able to overcome difficult material and, in many cases, that they were able to conquer their personal fear of failure.

In summary, students are unbalanced by teachers who challenge them. When teachers consistently act in a way different than students themselves do, the teacher's actions "unbalance" students. This proactive behavior by teachers fosters student change, growth, and learning.

Create a Classroom Environment in Which Failure Is Not Fatal

The social-educational environment is crucial to students' psychological well-being. Usually, an optimal environment is one in which students feel free to try new or different behaviors. Such an environment overcomes detrimental effects of the following myths that can effect learning (Lee, Pulvino, & Perrone, 1994a).

Myth 1: If You Work Hard Enough, You Can Accomplish Anything and Avoid Failure

This belief is false. Everyone fails at one time or another despite all their effort and talent. Failure is not always controllable. People may compete with others who are more talented. Environmental factors may affect performance. Most people are not geniuses! Despite hard work and practice, for instance, a person still might never be a concert musician. Failure is nature's way of indicating people's humanness and teaching them what they need to learn.

Myth 2: If You Fail, You Are Worthless

Failure is normal! Everyone, even the most successful people, fail from time to time. One's self-worth or value in the eyes of others should not be based on success or failure but on "how the race was run." Doing one's best and doing what needs doing, whatever the circumstance, should be the criteria for judging one's worth. Students, however, may have unrealistic expectations or work very hard to avoid failure. When they are not successful, the resulting negative impact can leave them feeling worthless. It is important for students to know that failure is a prerequisite for success. It provides the opportunity for increased learning and growth. Creative, productive, and successful people seem to develop a higher tolerance for their failures than do others. Such people are willing to learn from setbacks and refocus on what needs to be done to achieve the success they seek.

Myth 3: Failure Is Devastating

Failure is disappointing. However, in the face of failure, a person might tend to let feelings get carried away. When students experience failure as devastating, they become self-absorbed, turning inward. They often feel guilty because they did not work hard enough (myth 1) and start feeling worthless and create a negative cycle that builds on itself (myth 2). Even when trying to break the negative cycle and not being able to, students often jump to a second level of guilt and feel worthless because they are unable to control the negative cycle. Failure is to be accepted as a part of life, a valuable part that has potential for teaching important lessons.

Opposite the fear of failure is the desire for success. The strength of the fear of failure indicates the strength of the desire for success. Each carries the same weight to maintain some balance in the person's life. However, some people also fear success and may even consciously or unconsciously do things to ensure not succeeding.

It may seem contradictory to talk about a fear of success when most try to avoid failure. Students fearing success usually do something to sabotage their own efforts to succeed, even if they want to avoid failure. As with the fear of failure, several myths persist about the fear of success.

Myth 1: People Will Not Like Me Because They Will Think That I Think I Am Better Than They Are

Students often believe that if they are successful academically, others will shun them. Although some students do complain about "curve busters" or "teachers' pets," it is usually how an individual acts rather than their degree of success that determines whether others shun them. Thus, students who brag about their success are more likely to be ostracized than those who are happy with success but do not dwell on it.

Myth 2: There Is Too Much Pressure If You Succeed

Being successful is thought to bring with it added pressure to be even more successful—kind of a reverse of the fear of failure. Evidence supports the notion that when one consistently performs well, others will expect success all the time. Such a belief does not allow for the normal peaks and valleys of living. Successful athletes learn that they cannot give a peak performance every day or every game. Sometimes athletes feel on top of their game, and sometimes they have slumps. This is true for nonathletes as well. Fearing success because of the potential slump that might follow can initiate the slump without the joy of success. Further, every successful person has experienced plateaus in their development. Successful individuals accept plateaus as a normal part of development and patiently work through them. The fear of success may foster the very plateaus that the individual wishes to avoid.

Remember, success and failure are normal parts of life. Neither is to be feared or avoided, just accepted as part of life that provides valuable information that one can use for further learning. Teachers can help students be comfortable with success and failure by teaching them how to handle failure and success. Teachers can adapt the works of Carter and Kravitz (1996) for helping students deal with failure and success. They suggest that students can deal with failure by doing the following (p. 186):

1. Stay aware of the fact that you are a capable, valuable person.
2. Share your thoughts and disappointments with others.
3. Look on the bright side.
4. Explore why you failed.

Carter and Kravitz (1996, p. 188) offer the following advice for dealing with success:

1. First, celebrate.
2. Show yourself and others that the success is well founded.
3. Stay sensitive to others around you who may not have been so successful.

Finally, teachers can be most helpful to students by establishing learning environments in which both failure and success can occur without negative consequences. When students feel safe, they are more likely to attempt new or unfamiliar techniques and are more willing to take psychological risks. Psychological freedom is needed for personal growth. This can only occur in a safe learning environment in which fear of failure and success are minimal.

If Students Are Going Anywhere Near Where You Want Them to Go, Climb on the Bandwagon!

A positive attitude by teachers can be a great motivator. By acting as a cheerleader, teachers can encourage students to initiate action or continue movement if they have taken initial steps. When students are behaving in ways that you would like them to behave, reinforce their behavior. Consider the following example: Tim had been causing conflict in the classroom by failing to accept his responsibility in a small-group activity. The teacher, Mrs. Gladding, waited until Tim behaved in an appropriate way. At that point she reinforced his behavior.

MRS. GLADDING: It is important that each of you contribute to your group projects.

LISA: Not all of us have the same skills.

MRS. GLADDING: I agree with you. Yet, each of you can bring something unique to the group. As a group you have all the skills you need to accomplish the task.

LISA: I guess so.

TIM: Well, I'm not very good at figuring out all the angles on the drawing, but I can draw pretty good. I could do that part for the group.

MRS. GLADDING: Great, Tim! I'm sure you can; I've seen a number of your draw-
ings, and they were great. I'll bet your group will value your contribution.

Mrs. Gladding's simple response could encourage Tim to work with his group,
show the group that he was going to be an active participant, and add to the group
by providing a skill that others might not have. By responding in this manner, Mrs.
Gladding could make Tim feel more significant and encourage him to be an active
contributing member of his group. Bennis (1990) suggests that by responding to
people in this positive manner, they will feel "that what they do has meaning and significance" (p. 23) and, further, that this can help them feel empowered in the future.

Employ Models and Examples to Encourage Success

Teachers can encourage success by demonstrating useful models and by using examples of others' successes. By sharing how others have accomplished goals similar to
those being sought by the class, teachers can demonstrate methods for success. For
example, a mathematics teacher was confronted with getting her class to consider
how they might gain a visual understanding of equations. She asked a fellow teacher
who was skilled in using computerized mathematics programs to demonstrate alge-
braic equations on the computer. As a result of the computerized demonstration,
students better understood mathematical equations and their relationships. In addition, students were "turned on" to the computer and open to its use with other top-
ics. For instance, they were excited about how the computer could be used to solve
multiple equations, graph inequities, and solve area and volume problems.

Teachers also can use general examples to encourage success. For example, an
English teacher desirous of convincing her class that perseverance was an important
attribute of an educated person told her students about Einstein's inability to talk
until he was 5 years old, Churchill's early failures as a politician, and singer Mel
Tillis's stuttering problem. Another teacher, intent on demonstrating the power of
the subconscious mind in learning, discussed Edison's catnaps as precursors to a
number of his inventions. Still another teacher used artists Mother Moses and Anto-
nio Benedetti as examples of individuals who worked in obscurity for many years
before being recognized for their talent.

Teachers can use models and examples to demonstrate concepts and encourage
students. By following presentation of models and examples with appropriate discussion, teachers can provide students a basis for generalizing learning to other aspects
of their lives.

In summary, teachers can prevent conflict proactively. By unbalancing students'
normal way of learning by establishing high standards of excellence, creating a positive classroom environment, focusing on students' positive behaviors, and employing models and examples to encourage success, teachers can provide students a psychologically safe educational environment in which conflict will be the exception
rather than the rule.

USING FEEDBACK EFFECTIVELY

Feedback provides teachers a means for communicating their reactions to students' behavior and a way for shaping students' behavior in a positive direction. The concept of feedback "specifies that while sending or emitting a message, the sender is simultaneously receiving information related to that message or the environment" (Friend & Cook, 1992, p. 70). This definition suggests that feedback is an interactive process, one that uses verbal and nonverbal communication to link teachers and students.

Purposeful and careful use of feedback by teachers can help students achieve academically while feeling good about themselves. Effective feedback is the aikido principle of directing or redirecting student behavior. For effective feedback to happen, teachers should follow a few simple rules, which are addressed in the following subsections.

The Art of Feedback

Because the impact of teacher feedback can be great, it is important that it be used accurately and appropriately. The following four guidelines can be helpful.

Confirm the facts. It is important that data being used are valid and reliable before feedback is given. Teachers should use original sources of data and check for collaborating sources. When data cannot be verified, feedback must be given with caution.

Focus feedback on behavior, not motivations. Useful feedback is specific. Because of this, feedback should be focused on specific controllable behavior. It should not be focused on inferred motivations, underlying needs, or abstract reasons why students behave as they do.

Do it immediately. Most effective feedback is provided immediately after the behavior has occurred. If the time lag between behavior and feedback is too great, the impact of feedback is diminished.

Show your feelings. Feedback does not have to be provided without emotions. In fact, when teachers provide clear, specific, timely feedback with a measure of personal concern and/or passion, the message is more likely to be heard.

Recognize and Applaud Achievement

Feedback can be used for both positive and negative behaviors. When it is used to celebrate positive occurrences, teachers might consider the following:

Use every success as a cause to celebrate. No positive event is too large or small to celebrate. By responding to every positive success, teachers can help students identify the full range of their successes. This can provide students a more realistic perspective of their success and can help establish a solid foundation for personal self-worth.

Be specific with your praise. Make praise specific to the event being lauded. By being specific, students will know exactly what behavior(s) is warranting the positive feedback. This provides students clear, specific guidelines for the future.

Hand out commendations in public. Although some students might be embarrassed by receiving public praise, most will react favorably. Teachers should be aware of which students gain from public praise and which might benefit more from private feedback. In general, students feel good when they are singled out to receive positive feedback. Also, use of public praise has potential for secondary gains. First, other students become aware of the praised student's accomplishments. This effect establishes an expectation that the praised behavior will continue in the future and increases the likelihood that it will. Second, when others see one student receiving positive feedback, they are more likely to behave in a similar manner so that they also might receive positive feedback.

Employ some gesture to give weight to your commendation. The impact of positive feedback can be enhanced when teachers attach a **rider** to the feedback. For example, a rider that might go along with positive feedback might be that the student is allowed to do an extra-credit assignment, forego one homework assignment, or turn in a project 1 day late. Obviously, the rider should be consistent with the teacher's goals and the student's needs. The benefit of using this approach is that the praised behavior can result in intrinsic and extrinsic rewards for the student. This can foster continued motivation for positive learning behaviors.

Put your compliments in writing to be shared at home. The positive effects of feedback can be maximized by making sure that everyone important to the student is aware that the student has been singled out for praise. By sharing positive feedback, in writing, with the student's parents, teachers can enlarge the impact of the student's positive reinforcement by providing the student's parents a positive educational image of their child. This written sharing can help establish positive links among the student, teacher, and parents, which frequently results in long-term positive effects.

Employ a mixture of positive, negative, and intermittent reinforcement. Reinforcement through feedback can take on many forms. When students demonstrate wanted behaviors, positive feedback is the most appropriate. When they behave in unacceptable ways, negative feedback is needed. Yet, at times it may be best to use intermittent reinforcement. The value of this form of reinforcement is that it tends to perpetuate the activity being reinforced. For example, if a teacher wanted to encourage a student to work in groups, he might intermittently provide feedback to the student to encourage this behavior. In using all of these forms, it is helpful to be aware of the following possibilities.

Teach students to avoid certain behaviors, not you. It is important that teachers maintain a working relationship with students, especially if reinforcement is to be effective. The teacher-student relationship is essential for maximum learning to occur because it provides a base characterized by trust and caring. In this relationship, students can feel valued and are more likely to be open to constructive input. Students are more likely to listen to a teacher's feedback and to respond positively to what is suggested when a positive relationship is present. With a solid relationship, students are more likely to focus on the behavior under question and not on the teacher providing feedback about the behavior. By contrast, if a solid relationship is not formed, then a student is more likely to reject the teacher's inputs and/or the teacher.

Follow undesired behavior with immediate feedback. As stated earlier, feedback must be given immediately after behavior has occurred. By being timely with feedback, teachers can positively or negatively reinforce the *intended* behavior. When too much time occurs between behavior and feedback, the two variables may not be sufficiently associated in the student's mind. For example, if a teacher provided negative feedback to a student immediately after the student acted out in class, the student would know what prompted the feedback. However, if the teacher waited 3 days to give feedback, the student may not remember which specific behavior was being acknowledged. By waiting too long to provide feedback, the teacher can diminish or waste its impact.

Halt the negative feedback as soon as the negative behavior stops. The purpose of negative feedback is to provide input about a specific behavior or to help students stop an unwanted behavior. Therefore, teachers should use negative feedback only as long as the negative behavior occurs. Once the behavior stops, negative feedback should cease. If negative feedback is used beyond this point, it will negatively color the relationship, lead to loss of teacher credibility, and diminish potential positive effects of feedback.

If negative feedback is not working, try shaping absence of the behavior. In most cases, negative feedback is effective in reducing negative behavior. At times, however, negative feedback fails. When this happens, an alternate strategy that can be effective is to shape the absence of the behavior. For example, a student was continuously talking in class. The teacher tried to use negative feedback by responding every time the student demonstrated the unwanted behavior. Unfortunately, the teacher was unsuccessful in extinguishing the student's talking-out behavior. She decided to cease responding to the negative behavior and instead to positively reinforce the student when he did *not* talk out. This approach employs a positive perspective for shaping desired behavior and is a helpful alternative to using negative feedback.

In conclusion, feedback provides teachers an effective strategy for providing students input about and directing appropriate behavior. By careful and purposeful use of feedback, teachers can direct students' behavior while helping them achieve. In addition, effective feedback can provide a means for keeping lines of communication between teachers and students open. Obviously, this rapport is very important in conflict management.

USING THE POWER OF GROUPS

Groups hold great power. Educational classroom groups can be used to facilitate team building (Harshman & Phillips, 1994; Sanborn, 1992), decision making and problem solving, leadership, and creativity (Johnson & Johnson, 1991). Further, groups provide teachers a way to help students develop a number of important personal and social skills needed in later life, such as an opportunity to develop positive interdependence, face-to-face promotive interaction, individual accountability, interpersonal small-group communication skills, and group-processing opportunities (Johnson & Johnson, 1991, p. 2). Teachers can assure that students obtain these benefits and maximize their learning in group interactions by adhering to a few basic rules.

Place a Premium on Collaboration

Learning to work together is a primary task of group involvement. Teachers can facilitate this primary goal through their awareness of group structure and dynamics. For instance, by being aware that groups typically pass through developmental stages such as the security, acceptance, responsibility, work, and closing stages (Trotzer, 1977), teachers can anticipate how students will react as the group progresses. This awareness can help teachers maximize individual student learning while providing a psychologically safe group environment.

Teachers can use a number of specific strategies to assure that groups will be maximally effective.

Reward cooperation. Teachers can use feedback to communicate to students about their positive or negative group interactions. In general, teachers should use positive reinforcement when students demonstrate group cooperation and negative or intermittent reinforcement when they do not.

Assign responsibility for the group to the group itself. A group's personality is more than a total of personalities of individuals that comprise the group. Each group is greater than the sum of its parts. Each group is unique and tends to develop a personality of its own (Forsyth, 1990). Because of this uniqueness factor, the group must accept responsibility for the group. Consequently, group attitudes, decisions, and actions are all part of group responsibility. The teacher's task is to provide the group feedback on the degree to which it is responsible for its actions.

Plan learning tasks in which students must cooperate. By using group involvement interventions, teachers can help groups move through developmental stages and facilitate student involvement in the process. Interventions can be used that are stage appropriate. That is, specific interventions can be used that are most effective in security, acceptance, responsibility, work, and closing stages (Johnson & Johnson, 1991; Lee et al., 1994a).

Acknowledge and Use Community

The power of classroom groups was just discussed. Now, we turn attention to a larger group, the community. The community has power. For some students, it has great power; for others, less. Our intention in this section is to alert teachers to the potential influence of the community, not to elaborate on all aspects of that potential.

In Chapter 3, we discussed Hall's (1981) differentiation between high- and low-context cultures. It might be recalled that Hall suggested that German, Swiss, and Scandinavian cultures are very **low-context** cultures, whereas Chinese, Korean,

Japanese, and most African cultures are **high-context** cultures. A major point in Hall's treatise was that certain groups of individuals are more group oriented than others. That is, individuals from high-context cultures usually are more socially oriented than individuals from low-context cultures. They are more directly influenced by their community and less comfortable acting independently of that community. In a recent conversation, for example, an African-American graduate student described the difficulty that he had in leaving his hometown to go to college. He indicated a profound pull by members of his home community to refrain from going to college. He was able to overcome this pressure only because of a very strong countermessage provided by his mother. For this high-context-culture student, community pressure to conform to community standards and expectations was and is very great. He still must deal with formal and informal reactions to his decision whenever he encounters community members.

This example is not an isolated situation. Many students are confronted, daily, with pressures to conform to outside community standards. When the standards are consistent with classroom expectations, students have little problem. However, in those situations when community pressures and school standards differ, students can be caught on the horns of a dilemma. That is, which group do they respond to? If they respond positively to classroom standards, they run the risk of being ostracized by their community. If they respond to community standards, then they may have difficulty in the classroom. Conflict can be the end result—for the student, the classroom, or both.

Teachers can help alleviate this dilemma by recognizing its possibility, helping students understand the problem and its consequences, and proactively preparing to deal with it. How might teachers deal with a situation of this type? Although there are no easy answers, one approach that has been successful is to use representative community teachings to accomplish classroom goals. For example, Coleman and Bass (1996) report how a culturally relevant group intervention founded on principles from the African-American community was used with African-American male adolescents to reduce the risk for academic failure and underachievement. In this study, an Afrocentric rites of passage intervention using community-based principles of psychosocial development was practiced in the school environment to positively affect the academic achievement of 10 sixth-grade African-American males. This study indicates that adaptation of principles of development originating in a specific community subculture are promising for helping at-risk African-American adolescents to achieve in school environments. In addition, this study reveals a broader, positive message. It demonstrates that success can be achieved when focus is on areas in which the community and classroom have similar goals. By focusing on areas of similarity, not dissimilarity, community and classroom can be brought together.

Teachers can have a positive impact on conflict management by finding ways to use culturally relevant material to reduce dissonance between community and classroom. The study by Coleman and Bass provides a stimulus for how this might be accomplished.

In conclusion, group involvement is an important element in classrooms. Also, the greater community has impact on students. Teachers can use their knowledge of classrooms and community to help students use and respond to groups in ways that will enhance their education. When they are successful in doing so, the potential for conflict will be diminished.

SUMMARY

The purpose of this chapter was to focus on ways that teachers can proactively prevent conflict in the classroom by applying aikido principles in positive ways. Four major ways were discussed. First, it was suggested that teachers focus on students. This can be done by expecting the best from them, concentrating on students' strengths, helping students discover their hidden talents, capitalizing on their desire to succeed, and refraining from using competition as a motivator. Second, emphasis was placed on teachers' approach to the education process. A positive approach is characterized by establishing high standards of excellence, creating classroom environments in which failure is not fatal, reinforcing positive behavior, and employing models and examples to encourage success. Third, feedback was discussed, detailing the nature of feedback, the value of recognizing and applauding students' achievement, and uses of positive, negative, and intermittent feedback. Finally, the power of groups was highlighted, particularly placing a premium on collaboration and acknowledging and using community.

REFERENCES

Bennis, W. (1990). *Why leaders can't lead*. San Francisco: Jossey-Bass.

Carter, C., & Kravitz, S. L. (1996). *Keys to success*. Upper Saddle River, NJ: Prentice Hall.

Coleman, H. L. K., & Bass, C. K. (1996). A culturally relevant group intervention with at-risk early adolescents. *School Counselor* (in press).

Forsyth, D. R. (1990). *Group dynamics* (2nd ed.). Pacific Grove, CA: Brooks/Cole.

Friend, M., & Cook, L. (1992). *Interactions: Collaboration skills for school professionals*. White Plains, NY: Longman.

Gladding, S. T. (1996). *Counseling a comprehensive profession* (3rd ed.). Upper Saddle River, NJ: Prentice Hall.

Hall, E. T. (1981). *Beyond culture* (2nd ed.). New York: Bantam Doubleday Dell.

Harshman, C. L., & Phillips, S. L. (1994). *Teaming up*. San Diego: Pfeiffer.

Johnson, D. W., & Johnson, F. P. (1991). *Joining together* (4th ed.). Upper Saddle River, NJ: Prentice Hall.

Lee, J. L., Pulvino, C. J., & Perrone, P. A. (1994a). *Dynamic counseling*. Minneapolis, MN: Educational Media.

Lee, J. L., Pulvino, C. J., & Perrone, P. A. (1994b). *Dynamic counseling: Structured exercises*. Minneapolis, MN: Educational Media.

McGinnes, A. L. (1985). *Bringing out the best in people*. Minneapolis, MN: Augsburg.

Muro, J. J., & Kottman, T. (1995). *Guidance and counseling in the elementary and middle schools*. Dubuque, IA: Brown & Benchmark.

Rosenthal, R., & Jacobson, L. (1968). *Pygmalion in the classroom*. New York: Holt, Rinehart, & Winston.

Sanborn, M. (1992). *Teambuilt: Making teamwork work*. New York: Master Media.

Tracey, D. (1990). *Ten steps to empowerment*. New York: Morrow.

Trotzer, J. P. (1977). *The counselor and the group: Integrating theory, training, and practice*. Monterey, CA: Brooks/Cole.

Young, M. E. (1992). *Counseling methods and techniques*. Upper Saddle River, NJ: Merrill/Prentice Hall.

Index